# JUST SAY KNOW!

Understanding and Reducing the Risk

of Sexual Victimization

of People with Developmental Disabilities

## DAVE HINGSBURGER

Diverse City Press Inc. (La Presse Divers Cité Inc.)
BM 272, 33, rue des Floralies
Eastman, Quebec
CANADA  J0E 1P0

Hingsburger, David J.  (1952 -     )

Just say know: Understanding and reducing the risk of the sexual victimization of people with developmental disabilities.

ISBN 1-896230-00-8

1. Handicapped – Abuse of.  2. Handicapped – Abuse of – Prevention
3. Handicapped – Sexuality – Sex Education

II

# CONTENTS

**This book is dedicated to Dick Sobsey**

Dick's work regarding the sexual victimization of people with developmental disabilities is inspiring. While we have only met a few times, his work has had an incredible impact on me. His writings are housed on my bookshelf within easy reach. For the moments he has given me, I am honoured.

# Acknowledgements

**Angie Nethercott**, speaks with clarity and determination and understands what it is for people to have the right to love.

\* \* \*

**Kathy Hatzipetrakos**, embodies warmth and listens better than almost anyone I know.

\* \* \*

**Brenda Poirier**, a "lucky chance" that speakers get of meeting like minded people while travelling.

\* \* \*

**Barb Vyrostko, Debbie Richards, Saro Stranges, Terry Haslam**, are committed to the rights of people with disabilities to know about their bodies and their hearts.

\* \* \*

**Gail Saunders**, who believes that the job of an executive director is to support, not control.

\* \* \*

**Bruce** and **Shirley MacAuley**, who open their home for all who want to come. Even weary and often tiresome travelling lecturers can find a haven of warmth, welcome and occasionally, if very lucky, fresh donuts.

\* \* \*

**Donna McKrow** and **Nancy Wallace-Gero** who fight for safe environments for people with disabilities to live and work.

\* \* \*

**Michel Mombleau, Rita Paradis**, merci pour ton amitié; **Julie** et **Caroline Drouin**, merci de remplir notre maison de la vie à tous les mercredis.

\* \* \*

**Joe Jobes**, who is the major part of my Ring of Safety.

\* \* \*

**Erin Kaye**, my niece, who is brighter and more beautiful than she realizes. She did an excellent job of reviewing this manuscript.

# The Source

*You.* Sexual victimization is a subject that people avoid. The fact that you are reading this book means that you are part of the solution. I hope that you will get at least one "do-able" idea. If you do, then I have done my job. If you "do" the idea, then you have done yours. We all must do what we can when we can. Inaction in the face of inhumanity may be the greatest sin.

You never want the people you serve to say something like,

"Forgive them for they knew, but didn't."

# Introduction

We humans are so highly evolved.

*A herd of cattle*

Evolved past the need for others.

*A pack of wolves*

Evolved beyond the weakness of group membership.

*A school of fish*

Evolved beyond the animal desire for warmth and companionship.

*A crash of rhinoceroses*

Evolved beyond a primal drive for love.

*A kindle of kittens*

Evolved beyond the concept of responsibility and compassion.

*A hover of trout*

Evolved to the hatred of those we see as powerless.

*An unkindness of ravens*

Evolved to the concept of punishing weakness.

*A murder of crows*

Evolved to a celebration of the individual.

*An ostentation of peacocks*

Unlike "lower" creatures we have lost the desire to be ...

*A community of people*

# 1

## *WARNING:*
## *Toxic Attitudes Can Be Dangerous*

"Sex increases IQ."

I was stunned. A world famous sexologist stood in front of an audience and announced that a little 'bouncy bouncy' would boost brain power. My mind was working furiously on two different levels. At one very professional level, I was curious as to what clinical experience he'd had that would lead him to this kind of outrageous statement. Here he was in front of an audience of people who work with individuals who are developmentally disabled and he was making an absurd suggestion. At another much more personal level, I was hoping it were true and figuring that if masturbation counted I was growing brighter by the day.

He went on giving a brilliant lecture. He never explained the statement, he just meandered on to other topics as if what he said was so painfully clear that it didn't need explanation. He really wanted us to understand the importance of "sex role rehearsal play". He mesmerized the audience with slides of monkey teenagers having sex. It was hard to tell that the monkeys were teens because the animals seemed much more kempt and personable that any teenagers I happen to know. As the monkeys moved into mounting position you could feel the tension rise in the room and I realized that all these professionals were trying so very hard to be sophisticated and react in a purely professional manner. As I watched the mating scene on the screen along with his voice-over about "sex role rehearsal play", my mind kept returning to the idea of a link between sex and IQ.

When the male teen monkey was in position and was about to penetrate the female teen monkey, I wondered if this was animal pornography or merely erotica. I had heard about zoos that made erotic films of monkeys having sex to show to other shyer monkeys. I wondered if monkey porn stars had names like Kent and Kristie (with a heart used to dot the 'i'.) I wondered if the evolution happened because of the link between sex and IQ. I wondered if the missing link was some horny monkey whose IQ exploded during a weekend party that got out of control. I wondered why I hadn't been told this information when I was a teenager myself. I could imagine saying something like, "Honey I've got an exam tomorrow could you give me a hand?" It would at least have been more classy than begging for sex as a means of clearing up pimples!

Abruptly, almost prematurely, the slide presentation was over, lights came back on and the audience of social service workers had that uncomfortable-with-the-lights look on their faces but they all seemed inordinately proud of themselves for having gotten through the presentation. By the time the applause died down (which didn't take long because the sound of sweaty hands applauding is muted), I'm not sure that anyone else remembered the remark about sex and IQ. I did.

The crowd rose, as if one, and headed for the door. I escorted the esteemed lecturer to a cocktail reception held in his honour. We spoke very little, being a lecturer myself I knew that he needed quiet not company, so I simply guided him to the room. Once there, I asked him what he would have to drink and he requested a glass of wine. When I returned he was surrounded by people congratulating him for his frankness, his openness, his honesty, his comfort with the material but no one mentioned his slides and no one said anything that indicated that they had just witnessed the simian samba, the primate polka or the monkey minuet. Ah, how liberal we all are, we who walk upright. I did not drink as it would be my job to drive him to the airport.

Once in the car, I wanted to bring up the topic of sex increasing IQ. Considering the topic I wanted to sound bright. I wanted to sound like my IQ has occasionally shot up itself. When I brought the subject up, he said, "I wondered if someone would ask." He went on to say that he had had to be convinced to come and speak at this conference. He stated that the field of developmental disability is littered with prejudice and intolerance towards the very people we are paid to serve. I sputtered a protest. How could he? Didn't we just earn our liberality stripes by sitting in a room watching distant cousins bump uglies? He looked at me and asked if I wanted to hear a story.

He told me that he had not worked much with people with developmental disabilities not because he would not serve them, but because none were referred to him. One of the few situations he became involved with was with an agency that 'housed' people with developmental disabilities. They were in crisis. It seems that a young man and woman who lived in a group home had fallen in love with one another. When they announced their love and said that they wanted to get married, the news was not greeted with warmth and enthusiasm.

In fact, the front-line worker countered their news with news of her own. She informed them that the agency had a policy that essentially stated that people with disabilities who receive service cannot ever be sexual. Essentially, they were stating that if you were bright enough to have sex then you were too bright to receive service. What a dim policy!

The couple, having been informed that they would lose their home and their job for continuing their relationship, stated that they didn't care what anyone thought, they intended to marry. The front-line worker dutifully filled out an incident report. (It was probably the same form used to report aggression, toileting accidents and nocturnal emissions! We who watch, watch everything.) Once this act of agency treason had been reported the group home supervisor came in to counsel the couple. (For those new to the field, we use the word 'counsel' where others who love honest language would probably use 'browbeat', 'interrogate' or 'bully.') They were again informed that their relationship should it continue or become at all sexual would lead to an expulsion from their agency. They would lose home. They would lose job. They didn't care.

Now the reports were sent to head office. The residential manager called the couple in and informed them that their relationship was jeopardizing their placement. This was getting serious now and they had better come to their senses before something awful happened. They were prepared for something awful and wound up in the executive director's office. As they sat there and waited, you must realize that they sat on chairs that were paid for by their disability. The fact that they had a disability not only bought the furniture but the desk, the lamp shades and even the paper in the policy books. The man who spoke to them owed them his livelihood, his children's education and his breakfast! None of this was acknowledged for to acknowledge this big secret is to turn the pyramid upside down. As such they were spoken to as the problem rather than the employer.

The policy was read to them. There it was written clearly in wrong and right. Did they understand? They would lose their home. They would lose their job. The agency would HAVE NO CHOICE but to expel them. They said that they loved one another, wanted to marry and if that meant giving up their home and job then so be it. The executive director was ready for this level of non-compliance from them and asked them if they would be willing to see a doctor and let him help them make a decision. They said they were willing. They weren't unreasonable they were just determined. An appointment was set with the great doctor.

The doctor was foolish. He smiled when he admitted this and then glanced at me conspiratorially as if he let out his great secret. Yes it was possible even for experts to err. He actually believed that the agency was wanting to know if the couple was capable of marrying. It never crossed his mind as a possibility that someone would tell someone else that they couldn't marry because of who they are. So when he met them he felt that the tool that would be best able to assist him in assessing their capacity to understand commitment was the IQ test. But then he said that midway into the IQ test he realized something significant.

They made it into his office.

Do you realize what that means?

This couple stood up to a whole human service system and said "We don't care about your policies, we don't care about your punishment! We love one another and we are willing to sacrifice our home and our job to marry each other." The great, wise and all-knowing doctor was humbled in their presence. He said that one of the things wrong with modern love is that there is so little sacrifice any more. That two people were willing to completely sacrifice the comfort of the life that they knew for an uncertain future was incredibly moving.

He realized the decision had been made. A letter of support for the couple was sent to the agency. The agency reacted swiftly. The couple lost their placement. More than that, agency employees were told that if they continued to see the couple even in a friendly relationship they would be in a conflict of interest with the agency and they could be terminated. The couple's friends with disabilities who lived in the same agency were warned away from them. They were shunned by their past support system.

The couple married and moved into low cost housing in the downtown part of the city. The doctor was worried. Like any professional who gives politically correct but dangerous advice, it is difficult to see someone punished for doing what is advised. He arranged to see them again a year later. He noted that when they walked into his office they were not the same two people. They looked differently. They walked differently. They even spoke differently. Here they were standing in front of him after a year of living on their own. A year of supporting one another. A year of finding a non-paid network of support. A year of living with love in their lives. And it had made a difference. He performed IQ tests on them and he found that they had both increased.

Therefore, he said, sex increases IQ.

I must admit, I was disappointed. Clearly sex hadn't increased IQ. BUT... Maybe love did. Maybe pride does. Maybe freedom will. Maybe.

## WHY START HERE?

You may be wondering why a book on sexual assault of people with disabilities would start with a story that clearly is of love. And devotion. And commitment. A story that involves heart. And body. And soul. A story about pride. And strength. And determination.

This book begins here because there are rumblings out there in our field regarding sexuality and abuse of the people we are paid to serve. Every time new statistics that enumerate the countless thousands of people with disabilities that are raped, molested or otherwise sexually tyrannized are published, people meet in offices and shake their heads and wonder how to stop the abuse. While the discussion is admirable, it usually becomes a meeting which becomes a task force which becomes a policy that further outlaws people with disabilities from the possibility of being sexual.

## THE OTHER ABUSE

The agency that I have done most of my clinical work for has three different departments. One is for individuals who have a traumatic brain injury, one is for behavioural service towards individuals with developmental disabilities and one is the sexuality clinic which serves people with developmental disabilities who have engaged in inappropriate or deviant sexual behaviours. The community has become very aware of which department is which and referrals are targeted towards a specific part of the agency. Seldom do cross referrals happen.

One day I was called by a co-worker from the behavioural department. Now I would love you to be picturing a slickly beautiful office with intercoms, reception areas, and secretaries whose heels click click click down hallways waxed to a shine. In fact, our office is funded by human services and therefore is a basement office that battles moisture and mould and if my secretary's heels click click click anywhere they do on his own time. With that image clarified, you realize of course that when I say I was called by a co-worker I mean that they yelled down the hallway. I followed the voice to an office where I found a very concerned looking consultant.

She told me that she had a referral for an individual to be served by the behavioural team but that they felt that the referral really needed to be served through the sexuality clinic. I asked what the referral was for and I was told that it was for a man of about 40 years old who had toiletting difficulties. Toiletting?! Why would a referral be made to the sexuality clinic for toiletting? I was then told that the man seldom hit the toilet when he peed. I began to look suspi-

cious.  Was this a referral from my home for me?  In fact this referral could be made for most men.  It's kind of a guy thing to think that
your guy thing is a tad closer to the toilet than it really is.  I made
some probably tasteless remark and was sternly told to sit down.

The consultant from the behavioural clinic had begun work with
the individual and as part of a routine medical check it was discovered that this young man had wounds up and down his right thigh
and some scar tissue on his penis.  There was great concern that he
had been or presently was being abused.  The consultant was
requesting a consultation from the sexuality team and wanted an
assessment done that would help in determining if this fellow was
being hurt.  This was clearly a serious issue.

An appointment was set to meet with the client who seemed to be
pleasant and was unafraid of meeting me or looking at the assessment tool that we use.  Turning to the first picture in the assessment
kit, he was asked to point to an adult man and an adult woman.  This
he did with ease and he even talked about how he could tell they
were adults because they were taller and wore adult clothes.  The
next page is a line drawing of a naked man and he gave permission
for me to turn to the page.  He noticeably blanched when looking at
the picture.

"What is this called?" I said pointing to the eyes.  He was relieved
and answered confidently, "Eyes."  We went down the body, past
nose, past mouth, past chest and on to the belly button where he
began to tense up again.  Every answer was right, every answer was
solid, when I pointed at the penis on the picture and asked, "What is
this called?"  He turned his whole body away from the picture and
began to slap his hand saying, "*NO NO NO NO BAD BAD BAD
DIRTY DIRTY DON'T TOUCH DON'T TOUCH DON'T TOUCH.*"
There aren't enough exclamation points in the world to get across
either his volume or his pain.  This diatribe of anguish was the name
he had for his penis.  We uncovered years and years of having been
punished for touching his penis.

He had learned that that flap of flesh between his legs was filthy
and disgusting and was not to be touched at any cost.  A systemic
fear of masturbation had lead to abusive and hurtful teaching.  When

he would go to the bathroom he wouldn't touch his penis. He would use any object he could to dig it out of his pants. A pencil, that would do. A pen, sure that's fine. A knife, OK in an emergency. Then he would hold his penis on whatever object he'd used. When finished he would stuff his penis back into his pants with the object. This way he could pee without ever touching himself. He missed the toilet but he avoided punishment.

I wish I could tell you that our brilliant clinical work over-rode all the negative messages he had heard through his life. I wish I could say that our therapy put salve on the bruises that the slaps on his hands left on his soul. I can't. As far as we could get with him was to teach him to sit to pee. He will now roll toilet paper completely over his hand and then will push his penis between his legs. No he doesn't hurt himself any more, yes the wounds have healed on his legs and penis. But this is not an acceptable end to therapy but it was as far as he would let us go. Maybe with time. Maybe later. But maybe never.

This is the other abuse. The punishment of appropriate sexual expression is as abusive as any other form of assault. When an individual is taught that they, their feelings, their bodies, their hearts, their genitals are dirty, wrong, immoral, evil, profane or wicked, and when this message is taught through pain and punishment, then they have been sexually assaulted. It is as if their soul is pulled into the bushes and raped.

## PLAIN LANGUAGE

- The fact that people with disabilities are sexually victimized is never an acceptable rationale to write policies that forbid the possibilities of consenting loving relationships.

- The punishment of appropriate sexual expression is another form of sexual abuse. It involves someone in power misusing that power and assaulting an individual's development of a healthy sexual self.

## WHAT YOU CAN DO

- Avoid Overshadowing. There is a term called "Diagnostic Overshadowing" and it means that sometimes a doctor can't "see" a person past their disability. As such everything gets attributed to the disability. We all have seen this done by those outside the field, who hasn't heard a teacher complain that she wouldn't know what to do when a **retarded** child had a temper tantrum. As if the main issue was the disability not the behaviour. This is 'overshadowing.' We need to be aware of this because we do it too.

When visiting an agency recently they had a barbecue and invited me along. I told them that I was a vegetarian and asked if I could bring a tofu hot dog. They were shocked that I was a vegetarian because of their own diagnostic overshadowing ... fat people can't be vegetarian ... oh yes we can but we have to eat slowly and steadily. I expected the typical wrinkled nose at the idea of a tofu hot dog but I got an extreme reaction, not about the tofu, but about the hot dog! I couldn't bring a hot dog to a barbecue, what was I thinking! A hot dog!!??! I was completely thrown by the almost phobic response to the idea of a hot dog. I then was informed that some years, yes years, ago a person with a disability choked on a hot dog. Forgive me but I didn't get the connection and asked a probing question.

"Yeah, so?"

Well it seemed that the individual survived but could have died because of the attack of the killer hot dog. The agency called an emergency meeting. (Who pays these people?) They banned hot dogs. Now hot dogs are a controlled substance. Disabled people have to sneak out at night and meet strange people who peddle hot dogs on street corners if they want to indulge their criminal tastes! This is your brain ( O ) this is your brain on hot dogs ( * ) this is the brain of someone after a policy discussion about hot dogs in any form of meeting ( . ).

It is tragic but disabled people are people therefore they sometimes choke. It is tragic but disabled people are people therefore they sometimes fall. It is tragic but disabled people are people and therefore they sometimes are assaulted. All of these things are unfortunate but these things happen to people. Attributing an accident to a disability rather than a situation is diagnostic overshadowing. If we attribute every accident or mishap to a person's disability we wouldn't let them breathe-there are chemicals in the air. Besides passing policy on someone's life because of a tragedy is a subtle way of blaming the victim and trying to protect them from themselves.

- Define Appropriate Sexual Behaviour. Make sure that your agency comes to some kind of agreement about what appropriate sexual expression is allowed. Even if they don't want to write a policy about sexuality, it is important to make sure that they at least come to a consensus about masturbation. If they don't, then inconsistency will reign because some staff will ignore, some staff will encourage but some staff will punish. Beyond being very confusing, people with disabilities will be dealt with by the whim or belief of any staff who works with them.

- Investigate policy statements. While on the road I did some training in Springfield, Massachusetts, for the Association for Community Living. I met Pat Carney who was part of a team of people putting together a policy regarding sexuality and people with disabilities who live in residential settings. They gave it to me to review. It was absolutely brilliant. They have just published it and I would strongly recommend that you purchase it to see how they have structured their policy. The reference is in the list of resources at the end of this book.

Even if you have policy in place, remember policy should change and grow. If you don't re-evaluate policy every couple of years then it becomes a rigid code rather than a flexible set of standards that reflects a changing population and changing times.

- Never say, "The system can't change."

In his amazing book, *Obedience to Authority*, Stanley Milgram coined a term that I had never heard of before. In fact I can hardly say it now. The term is "Antianthropromorphization." How's that for alphabet soup. We all have engaged in some form of anthropomorphization which is the giving of human characteristics to non-human objects. Saying that a tree is "lonely" is attributing human emotions to a non-human. Dr. Milgram thought it was important to understand the opposite or the "anti" of that which is the taking away of human characteristics from human things.

When people talk about the "system" they usually do so as if the system were concrete and non-human. This isn't the case, the "system" is you and me. It is a human creation that can be changed almost at will. Seeing an "agency" as unchangeable is assuming that the "agency" exists independently of all those who work in it. It does not. An agency and a system "is" the people who work in it.

Please remember this fact when reading this book. We are the system. If we change, so does the system, at least a little bit. When you read something that you think needs to be done but that the "system" won't allow it. Stop and ask instead, "Who do I need to talk to about this?"

By the way, if someone tells you that change can't happen "Because that's the system." Look them straight in the eye and say, "Your thinking is a tad antianthropomorphic don't you think?" If you have a ten dollar word, you might as well use it!

## SUMMARY

It was Saturday morning. The buses and cars were dropping off a large number of people with developmental disabilities who were coming to a day long session on how to say "NO!" I was meeting with two women who were learning how to run the workshop in a small room just off to the side of the auditorium where the workshop was to begin. All the advertising stated that staff and caregivers were not invited to the workshop. When one of the women went into the auditorium she found 60 people with disabilities in a variety of groupings talking together about any number of topics. Off to the side sat a young staff who sat alone and looking more than a little perturbed.

Thinking that the staff didn't understand that the workshop was restricted to people with disabilities, she approached her and asked if she intended to stay. The staff stated that she had no intention of staying but was waiting for us to show up because there was no-one in the room.

"No-one was in the room." A roomful 60 people was seen as empty. When she was informed that there were a lot of people in the room. The staff, not getting it, said, "Well, now that there's some-one here, I can go."

WHAT?

Oh yeah.

Antianthropomorphization.

Taking of human characteristics away from human beings. The first step in the long road of oppression, prejudice and abuse.

# 2

# *The Prison of Protection*

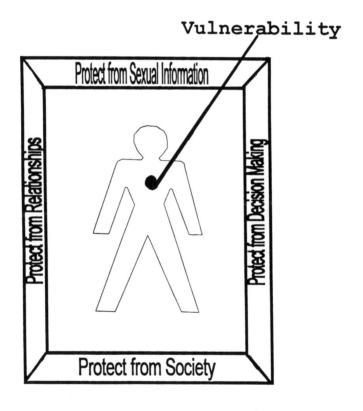

Annette was raped in her own home by her brother-in-law.

Let me tell you about her life before the rape. She had the picture perfect life. By her definition. Her family had lived for years in the downtown core of the city. Annette worked at a sheltered industry where she felt valued and an important part of a work team. She loved the work, her co-workers and her instructors. She rode the handi-trans from a home wherein she was loved to work which gave her day meaning. We should all be so lucky.

Her family had set a goal for itself. They wanted to move from the downtown core to a suburb where many people from their ethnic group lived. As a family they scraped and saved. The day that they could move was celebrated with joy. The family, and Annette, were naive about human services and thus were shocked to find that once they had moved Annette could no longer attend her sheltered industry. They had moved across one of those invisible geographic boundary lines that determine which agency owns which population of people with disabilities. Annette would have to change jobs.

She made the visit to the new sheltered industry and found the work boring and the atmosphere oppressive. She didn't want to work there. In fact, she no longer wanted to live in the suburb. Annette felt that moving back downtown was the solution. You may be thinking that she should have moved on her own, but Annette did not want to leave her family home. She simply wanted them all to move back downtown so she could go back to work. This would be impossible. She called a staff from the sheltered industry and expressed her dissatisfaction with the way her life had changed.

This staff spent time convincing others at the sheltered industry that Annette was such an asset to the workshop that she should be allowed to return to work. In a rare flash of compassion from an organizational team asked to re-evaluate its policy, Annette was told that she could come back to work even though there would be no funding dollars attached to her. The difficulty was transportation. There was no way that it could be arranged for her. She would have to learn to come on her own.

Annette was an enthusiastic learner. She had a goal in mind and she met it. Within days she had learned the transit system enough to take the bus, two subways and walk several blocks to work. She was thrilled to be back at the job she loved. The only fly in the ointment was the pay. She felt that she didn't earn quite enough money at the sheltered industry. One evening when her mother was visiting with a friend who was complaining about the difficulty of working and keeping house, Annette offered to work one night a week cleaning house. Ironically she made more from that one evening cleaning house than she did for two weeks working at the sheltered industry. She was rich beyond money. A job she loved. A home full of love and support. Extra money when she needed it.

Annette was raped in her own home by her brother-in-law.

After the rape. Annette's life changed. Her parents were distraught and angry decisions were made. Annette was no longer seen as a competent young woman, she became a "victim" she became "vulnerable" and they decided that she could no longer ride the transit, go to work or walk through the neighbourhood. She was to be kept at home where she could be watched at all times. She was to be protected.

It was difficult talking with Annette's family. They were firm. She was to be kept safe at all cost. Even if that cost was personal liberty. Trying to point out to them that their decision did not make sense was impossible. Finally, it had to be said.

Annette was not raped on the transit system.

Annette was not raped at the workshop.

Annette was not raped in the neighbourhood.

Annette was not raped while cleaning house.

Annette was raped in her home, where she is now prisoner.

While the family's decision may seem harsh, it is the decision that is often made when we change our view of someone as competent to someone who is vulnerable.

## DANGEROUS WORDS

Vulnerable is a dangerous word. It is now used to describe a state of being and as such one hears of "Vulnerable Populations." This is making "vulnerability" a character trait of a particular person or a particular group of persons. It is laying the blame for the victimization inside the person. If we believe that someone is assaulted because of who they are then there is no option but to protect them because nothing can be done to alter their state of being. Annette is and will remain a person with a disability. If the disability caused the assault then the source of the assault is lodged somewhere inside her.

Victim is a dangerous word. To say that someone is a victim is to say that their state of being has been altered by the act that was perpetrated on them. To say that Annette is a victim is to say that she is now and she will ever be seen differently by those who regard her. As a victim she can never again be seen as separate from an act which was done to her.

## PRISON WALLS

The prison of protection is built of kindness. When we as service providers see someone as being 'vulnerable' because of who they are we become protectors. There are four walls to the prison. The walls are built to protect the person, who is seen as vulnerability encased in flesh.

## PROTECTION FROM SEX EDUCATION

I keep waiting for it to happen. With every newscast about AIDS and other sexually transmitted diseases, I expect it to happen. With every published report regarding the victimization of people with developmental disabilities, I am sure it will happen. With every panicked call from an agency dealing with unwanted pregnancy, I assure myself it will happen. But often it doesn't. Sex education is still a contentious topic. People still worry that sex education is going to fan the flames of wanton lust. (As if that's a bad thing!) People tell me that the problem IS sex education. I am assured that people with developmental disabilities just won't understand.

Oh to be sure, it's gotten better. More and more agencies are seeing the need. But there is a huge problem. Whenever I do a workshop about sexuality or sex education the audience is almost completely comprised of staff who work with adults with a developmental disability. It seems that we will grudgingly provide education to adults, but the question of providing education to children with disabilities is still verboten.

Because sex education has become known as a "tab A into slot B" phenomenon, parents think that sex education is something that begins when children start to wonder about their "tabs" and "slots." Sex education needs to be seen as something that is more encompassing and less focused on genital geography. Parents of kids with developmental disabilities often wonder when, if ever, it is appropriate to teach their children "sex ed." They worry that by bringing the subject up they will go too fast or confuse their children by omitting morals and focusing on behaviour or the reverse. These concerns are valid especially if the child is first introduced to sex in their late teens or early adulthood because a lot will need to be taught very quickly.

Sex educators recommend that sex education begin very early. This often leaves parents with the vision of sitting down with a child barely out of diapers teaching them about sexual intercourse. Parents would be rightly horrified if that is what we, as sex educators, meant. I too, agree that sex education needs to begin early, but I see sex education as teaching about gender and privacy, as well as social and affectional skills. This might be better understood if we understood better the normal socio-sexual growth of children.

To do this let's look at the development of understanding of sexual behaviour of typical children up to the age of 7. This will give an idea of how much ground has to be covered and the type of concepts that children need to learn before they get to the "critical" items such as sexual dreams, ejaculations, and menstruation, all of which can be traumatic with no information or preparation.

Infancy to Two Years Old: Children have a capacity to show a sexual response from birth. Both boys and girls engage in some pleasurable sexual self-stimulation. At this age it is important that parents not punish the behaviour although they may wish to re-direct it when the child is in public. The key issue here is that this is normal behaviour and not a sign of a child being oversexed or abused. The most important concept that is learned in this period is gender. By age two and a half most children know what gender they are, even though they do not have a sense of "gender constancy" which is the understanding that they will always be the gender they are. Many children at this age think they are girls today but may be boys tomorrow. This is primarily because they understand gender by clothing, haircuts and behaviours which are transient.

Three to Seven Years Old: There is a marked increase in sexual behaviour, specifically masturbation. There is also an increase in sexual play between children. Again, these are normal behaviours and parents need to respond with calm when the behaviours occur. The main issues are those of privacy and consent. (While it is normal for children to play doctor, it is important for them to understand that they cannot force others to play the game with them.)

The most important concepts which are learned during this period are those of marriage, familial relationships and gender constancy. Children form an understanding of loving bonds between people and they learn that their gender is determined by their genitalia and that this is a non-changing part of who they are. Probably most importantly they learn the principle of modesty (body privacy) by the age of seven.

What does this mean to parents of kids with disabilities: This means that all parents, including parents with disabilities, need to understand that children engage in various forms of sexual behaviour from infancy and that this needs to be accepted as normal development. But more importantly, parents of kids with disabilities need to understand that there are concepts that must be taught during this period to keep their children on a normal developmental track: gender (as defined by outward characteristics), gender constancy (as defined by genitalia), socio-sexual relationships like marriage and modesty. All of this learning is pretty impressive but when you add to this knowledge the fact that the child has somehow learned that their body is private and that they want to be the ones to determine if the door is open or closed, you realize how far kids have come in those few years.

**Why Protection is Dangerous**

You can see that typical children have a number of concepts that will keep them safer. They understand modesty and privacy. They understand relationships and appropriate touch within those relationships. But they have something more, they have language. Protection from sex education leaves a person effectively mute when it comes to speaking of their body. Imagine that someone is attempting to touch your vulva and you don't want it touched, how could you tell someone if you had no language? Imagine that someone is sticking his hand down your pants and fondling your penis, how do you tell someone if you don't know the words? How? You can't.

The gay community has been very effective in getting the message across about AIDS. Many people have seen people wearing black tee shirts with the slogan SILENCE = DEATH. I believe that the slogan for people with disabilities should be LANGUAGE = POWER. You must realize that if you oppose sex education for people with disabilities you are also opposing language development. A dramatic case which emphasized the need for the language of sex was reported in the newspaper some years ago.

A young boy had a tumorous growth on his testicle that was causing him great pain. His parents noticed his behaviour change, but he said nothing. His performance in school deteriorated, but he said nothing. Eventually, when taken to the doctor the growth was discovered. When he was asked why he didn't tell anyone he said that he didn't know what to call it. Oh, he knew that other kids call them "balls" but he knew that wasn't the word and there was no way he could say the word "balls" to his mother. Language training does more than give language it demystifies the language so that it can be spoken.

To a certain degree the desire to prohibit sex education is the fault of how sex education has been advocated. Usually it is talked about from the perspective of a person's right to be sexual. While this is true, I think it steps far past the initial benefits of sex education. Parents, and those who care for children with developmental disabilities, need to realize that when we advocate sex education for children with developmental disabilities we are advocating for a thoughtful approach that teaches the right skills at the right time.

## PLAIN LANGUAGE

• When people with disabilities are denied access to sex education they become perfect victims because they can't report what they can't say.

• Sex education needs to begin early and teach, concept by concept, the things that all children need to learn in order to be safe, feel good about, and understand themselves as sexual beings.

## PROTECTION FROM DECISION MAKING

Years ago when I was involved in the deinstitutionalization movement I took a man, who had been confined for most of his life, on an outing. His access to the community had been limited, not because of his behaviour or his ability, but because he had been passive. He hadn't minded staying back and letting others go. As a result he seldom had left the grounds of the facility. I tried to think of somewhere interesting to take him and ended up taking him to an ice cream store that advertised 40 billion different flavours. I figured I would introduce him to my world, a world full of wonderful options and choices. A world full of flavours and smells. A world full of empty calories and food with no nutritional value.

I remember standing there with him in the store. His face was pale in the bright neon white lighting. Others scurried by us ordering things like death by chocolate, vanilla-cherry swirl, peanut butter parfait, and other fancy ice creams. He was lost. I tried reading him the list and getting him to choose but he couldn't. He had never had so many choices. He didn't know how to make the decision. I realized that for him choosing one was losing all the others. He had no concept for doing what I asked him to do. He couldn't make a decision.

My first time on a radio show as an invited guest was to talk about sexuality and developmental disability. I was naive, a talk show virgin, and I approached the show with excitement. When talking to the host of the show during the commercial break before going to air he was such a nice guy. I was lulled into a sense of security. But when the commercial was over so was the charade. He attacked me! He said something like, "OK, Mr. Hingsburger you are coming into this community, as a guest of Planned Parenthood – and we know what kind of organization they are, to advocate for the right for people with developmental disabilities to have sex. Let's get it straight for my listeners. I know that in "new speak" developmental disabilities is the new word, but let's be honest, shall we? You are advocating that retarded people can have sex? Is that right?"

He was using a strategy that I have come to know well, using a lot of words and make a statement while asking a question that has only a one word answer. I answered, "Yes." It was frustrating because I didn't have an opportunity to explain my point of view before he continued. "Now Mr. Hingsburger, how can you advocate that people who can't even balance a checkbook should have the right to have sex?"

An opening. I responded, "Sir, if you are suggesting that only people who can balance a checkbook should be able to have sex, then I ask you, Who would get to do it?" That stopped him. His ignorance I can forgive. I mean he is paid to be ignorant. But when I hear this kind of sentiment from people who work with disabilities I am a lot more worried. Let's acknowledge that many people with developmental disabilities, like the man in the ice cream store, have difficulty with decision making. This I grant you. But I think that most of the difficulty is because of lack of practice rather than lack of ability.

Let's take a trip through your developmental history as you learned decision making. When you were born, and such a beautiful baby I'm sure, your parents made all decisions for you. This is a period of time they liked. Then come the terrible two's when you learned that your thoughts and actions could run counter to what your parents said. Don't touch that vase? Right. CRASH. As you got older you began to want in on the discussion about your bed time, your allowance, your friends, your food, eventually you were fighting about everything.

21

What was happening is that as you grew and became more competent, you were taking over the decision making skills for yourself. So by the time you left home you had years and years of decision making practice behind you. Your parents had systematically taught you about making decisions. I'll bet you can even remember a time when your parents let you make a wrong decision. They knew it was wrong, they knew you would get hurt, but they also knew that you had to learn about consequences. They probably didn't realize that they were teaching you how to make a decision, but they were.

For you to see yourself as competent as a decision maker because you were born that way is unfair to the work your parents put into you. The very first time you looked at your parents and howled something like, "WHEN I GROW UP I'M NEVER, EVER, EVER GOING TO EAT PEAS AGAIN", you were saying, even as a child that you could envision a future where you would make decisions about your life. Unfortunately, many people with disabilities are still "eating peas" because they never grew into a state of independence that would allow them such freedom.

## WHY PROTECTION IS DANGEROUS

It is tempting to attribute decision making difficulties that some people with disabilities have to their disability. Often this is simply diagnostic overshadowing. The belief that people with disabilities are inherently vulnerable and the fact that they are vulnerable because of the disability seem self evident have lead to a situation wherein staff feel that they should do all of the cognitive work for a client. Why? Well they are cognitively disabled aren't they? They are vulnerable aren't they? Then they are vulnerable because of their minds, wouldn't you say? Then let's never let them use their minds. We will protect them from their own damaged minds, that will keep them safe!

The end result of this is people who don't know how to make a decision. People who think that their job is to second guess staff, and try to guess what is wanted from them. Once, when asking a person with a disability if she liked the roller coaster, I threw her into a quandary. We had never talked about this before. She had no idea if I liked or disliked the roller coaster. She tried to read my face for the right answer. She didn't understand that I wanted her to tell me what she liked not what I liked.

## PLAIN LANGUAGE

• People with disabilities often have difficulty with decision making because they have no practice at decision making.

• As a result, adults with developmental disabilities are being asked to make decisions about big things, like sex, without understanding big consequences, like disease, before they learn to make decisions about little things, like peas, without learning little consequences, like hunger.

• The ability to make up your own mind is the first step on the way to autonomy and the ability to say, "No!"

## PROTECTION FROM SOCIETY

Just get in a car and drive to where people with developmental disabilities have been congregated. Please judge the place not the people who work there or the people who live there. I have found tender kindness among staff who work in places with corridors a mile long. I have found people with disabilities who have made those places into places of community and comfort. Judge instead the attitude that built the building in the first place.

The idea that all human beings grow and develop does not seem to be a radical one. Yet it is quite a revelation to many that all humans have the capacity for learning. The idea that people with developmental disabilities can learn still astounds many. The evidence of this astonishment can be seen in newspapers all over the United States and Canada as parents require that schools provide educational service in regular classrooms to those who have been seen as 'uneducable' or barely 'trainable.' The fight for the regular classrooms and community living can be better conceptualized as the fight for context.

The area of human development the theory that has most effected my work has been that of "context." The simple idea that people learn from their environments and their social interactions within those environments has had a tremendous impact. Years ago it was felt that 'special' environments needed to be created for 'special' people. As such, those who were considered different intellectually were herded into large institutions where they received custodial care. If children can be said to learn what they live, a generation of people with developmental disabilities learned indifference, learned segregation, learned abandonment and learned prejudice. More than all these things, statistics now tell us that they learned abuse.

If indeed people learned from their environments, would that explain some of the behaviour of people who have lived their lives with no stimulation? Is it possible to see the shuffling gait of a person who had never walked free of institution halls as a result of the shackles of inactivity and inattention? Is it possible to see self injurious behaviour as an individual simply internalizing and "physicallizing" an attitude of hatred for disability. If this is true then a human tragedy was in the making.

My first job working in the community was in an experimental group home where we moved people from the back wards of a large institution into a small group home in the center of a city. We had an incredible job. We were simply to expose people who hadn't set foot in the larger community to day to day living experiences. More than that we were paid to create a family atmosphere wherein respect, caring and attention were definable characteristics.

As we did this, professionals came in with videocameras and made tapes where they could compare the behaviours, skill levels and emotional states of these folks to those they exhibited in the institution. We, staff, were not allowed to see the 'before' tapes as it was felt that we might target our teaching to assure a positive outcome from the experiment. When the study was done, results tabulated, articles written, we were invited to a day of watching the 'before' tapes of the individuals that had become our family.

We were awestruck and many staff, myself included, cried quietly as we watched our residents, our friends, in a much different context than the one in which we met them. Seeing people showering in huge rooms, sleeping forty to a room, having food shoved into their mouths, and grasping for attention we were stunned. The people we knew were not these people. The skills we had taught them in our 'action plans' had been achieved. The hand washing, cooking, dressing kind of rudimentary skills which occupied so much of our time had little impact on the before and after tapes. What stunned us was not skills but attitudes! The people we knew walked with pride, dressed with care, groomed for approval, smiled and responded to social cues. We had not programmed this motivation. We had never intended to teach self-respect and, in effect, we hadn't. From the understanding of human development, what we saw was people drawing from the context of home and the introduction to the context of community.

Today, years later, these same people who had spent their day in meaningless activities have conquered new contexts. They work, some at relevant tasks in sheltered employment, others at artistic and leisure skills and still others in competitive employment. The success of these people and thousands of others have fuelled a movement which was initially called, "Normalization", where social service activists and parent advocates fought and continue fighting to allow people with developmental disabilities to grow up in regular environments. Children belong at home, the disability is irrelevant. Children belong at school, the disability is irrelevant. Children belong in neighbourhoods, the disability is irrelevant.

It is intriguing to now be meeting young people with developmental disabilities who are in their teen years and have never been outside normal contexts. They have been integrated into regular schools, lived with a normal peer group and have had the benefit of being parented at home in their natural communities, what a difference! If anything has made the point of the effect of "context" on human development this new generation does. They read! They have dreams! They want to share themselves and their lives with others! It is hard to imagine that if they had been born a generation earlier, they would be found now curled in the corner of an institution waiting as leaden minutes pass for the meal cart to be wheeled onto the ward.

The issue of sexuality cannot be separated from the issue of segregation. There is no denying that the "differentness" of people with disability leads people to fear, and in this case the fear is based, at

25

least partially, on attitudes towards the sexuality of people with disabilities. There are essentially two differing views of people with disabilities and their sexuality. The first is, "They are sexually innocent and need to be protected from a dangerous society." The second is, "They are sexually dangerous and the innocent in society need to be protected from them." Both these views are commonly seen but the second one is the more prevalent. Anyone who has tried to open a group home in a neighbourhood has come up against neighbours worried about the safety of their children. Whenever someone says something like that, you know that they are saying that "These strange retarded people are going to move in here and molest our children."

I had a lot of trouble reconciling the two views until I realized that it didn't matter which view you held, segregation was the only answer. They are sexually innocent so segregate them from society. They are sexually dangerous so segregate them from society. Both views build institutional walls. And institution walls define the context in which people live their lives.

## WHY PROTECTION IS DANGEROUS

Let it just be said that the deeper a person is in the human services system, the more likely it is that they will be abused. Let it also be said that people learn what they live and in order to live free one must have been free, in order to live proud, one must have experienced pride.

## PLAIN LANGUAGE

• Difference is never a reason to lock people away from society.

• People with developmental disabilities are neither inherently sexually innocent nor inherently sexually deviant.

• Living free and proud is a right of every citizen of a civilized society.

## A SMALL IRONY

Oddly, people are taught to fear strangers. One of the most commonly taught strategies for avoiding sexual victimization may backfire. "Don't talk to strangers!" Who hasn't heard that message? This is taught with the best of intentions but it may be a dangerous concept to teach. It further separates people with disabilities from the society at large in that they fear all those outside the system while they are abused by those within the system. Like other groups who are highly victimized, people with disabilities have more to fear from those they know than those they don't.

One man was abducted from a mall and while he struggled he never once called out for help. When asked why he didn't ask for help he said that he looked around and all he saw was strangers. He knew not to talk to strangers. He was raped. He followed a rule he learned to protect him and he was hurt. He needed to learn that there are times when every stranger is a potential friend. Since that incident I have begun teaching a different concept. After another class with people with disabilities wherein I asked the question, "Is it OK to talk to a police officer, if the police officer is a stranger?" The answer? An unqualified and unanimous, "No!" Time for a new concept.

I remembered talking to a friend of mine, Linda Hickey, years ago who told me that she had taught her son that strangers were OK but that he was to be careful of people who act strangely. She placed the focus of her son's training on the behaviour not the person. She used lots of examples: It's strange when someone you don't know wants to give you something. It's strange when your uncle wants to touch a private place. It's strange when your teacher wants you to touch their private place. It's strange when your friend threatens you not to tell that they hurt you. THIS IS A VERY TEACHABLE CON-CEPT. (The capital letters is for those of you who just went "pshaw!")

Teaching that strangers necessarily equal danger further separates people with disabilities from the society we aim at involving them in. It's quite a neat trick for those who would abuse their positions of trust to teach people with disabilities a lack of trust in others!

## PROTECTION FROM RELATIONSHIPS

He was referred to us as a child molester. Those two words are amongst the most horrid in our society. But he had been observed staring at children, particularly young girls. He had also been caught masturbating while watching television shows with young female actors. His agency was concerned. While his disability was such that he required a fair degree of supervision, they wondered as to the potential he had for harming another. An opinion was requested.

I hadn't met with him for long, before I noted the behaviour that concerned everyone. When driving with him, his eyes would leave the road and scan residential yards. He always seemed to be look-ing. When he caught sight of a young girl his face would become transfixed and a dreamy look would appear in his eyes. His arousal showed on his face. When anyone tried to redirect him from his stare he could become quite aggressive and had put at least one staff in the hospital.

Convinced that he was a pedophile, he was accepted into our ser-vice. Work began by gathering a history and reviewing his file. The incident reports that had accumulated in his file were nothing less than damning. For years he had been seen in situations that, if he were unsupervised, would have undoubtedly lead to an offense. He was dangerous. The file was mute regarding any appropriate sexual expression and I was growing very worried about this man's danger. It seemed that whenever there was an opportunity (when staff weren't directly supervising him) he would assault anyone. Man, woman, or child, no-one was safe.

Having determined that he needed to be formally tested to deter-mine his sexual arousal patterns, he needed to be informed of peo-ple's worry and thus have the need for the test explained to him. Driving him back from my office to his workplace, there seemed to be a moment when I could present this issue to him. He caught him-self staring at a child and, having being warned so often to look away from children, he self-corrected and guided his eyes back to the road. This seemed to be a moment of self discovery so I brought up the test with him.

He seemed confused about the test and wanted clarification. I told him that people were worried that he was sexually attracted to chil-dren. This information had no impact so I said that we wanted him to become more attracted to adult women. This information did have impact.

"THAT'S STUPID!!!" He was very angry. I pulled the car over as I have a rule that when there is yelling there should be no driving. Why was he so angry? I asked him to explain why it would be "STUPID!!!" to be attracted to adult women. Then he told me his story.

He moved into a community group home from his family home. He said that he was only there for a short time before he noticed a young woman who had really noticed him. He said that he liked her and she liked him. He knew that the staff couldn't know about it or they would get angry. Their love grew in the shadow cast by intolerance. They sat beside each other on the bus to work and would hold each other at the dances that were held in the auditorium of the facility nearby.

He became more agitated when talking about when he kissed her and how much he liked to be near her. I wish you could have been in the car with me to see and hear him tell this story. This is the story of first love. It was not told with longing. His body didn't relax with the telling. It was told with anger and his body was taut. He mentioned having sex with her. I must have communicated my discomfort with this disclosure to him because he glared at me and said, "Sometimes she came to me first." He had read my mind. He knew that I automatically worried about consent. Without even having to ask, he told me that they both initiated the contact.

Where did their loving take place? In the hallway down in the basement of the group home. They would sneak away while staff were busy upstairs and meet downstairs. They were not dumb. They knew that staff would follow certain routines at certain times. They knew when to escape the glare of supervision.

One of the staff must have broken with routine and discovered them downstairs. He reported being pulled off top of her and sent to his room without dinner. (Yes we are talking about an adult man here.) And when he left his room in the morning he discovered that she was gone. Her room was empty. She wasn't at the workshop either. Suddenly she was ready for community employment. He never saw her again.

Then he asked, "What difference does it make who I touch, people get mad?"

Until I could answer that question, no therapy was possible.

## WHY PROTECTION IS DANGEROUS

Protection created a dangerous offender. To him, all sex is wrong so it doesn't matter if it's an adult or a child. It doesn't matter if it's consenting or if it's rape. It doesn't matter if it's public or private. It doesn't matter if it feels good or if it hurts. Sex is wrong plain and simple. This loss of "figure-ground" leaves a person with a disability unable to distinguish "good sex" from "bad sex."

There are two tragic consequences to this. The first is that a person, thinking all sex is bad, will simply assault someone when they feel aroused. To them there is no appropriate time, place or person, there is simply a desire that needs to be expressed. The second is that a person who is overpowered by another and whose will is taken away while that other sexually abuses them will never tell. To them a sexual act has occurred. They will see themselves as having been involved in something terribly wrong and will see themselves as culpable. To say that they were involved in something sexual is to admit that they were bad, dirty or sinful.

## PLAIN LANGUAGE

• Oppression of natural sexual desire and natural sexual behaviour leads to other, more serious, problems.

• The denial of appropriate relationships robs people with disabilities of the ability to discriminate between that which is acceptable and that which is not.

• People who are victimized will fear being punished for doing something sexual and therefore will not come forward.

### *WHAT YOU CAN DO*

• Examine your attitudes. How do you respond to the idea of sexually appropriate behaviour and the clients you support. (Don't opt out of this if you work with those who have severe or profound handicaps!) Does the idea that they might masturbate make you uncomfortable? Does the thought that they might kiss each another horrify you?

I want you to imagine for a moment that you walk into your living room at night after supper. You have been in the dining room and when you enter the living room you notice that the television set has been left on but there is no-one else in the room. The music that accompanies the program attracts your attention and you sit down in your favourite chair to watch the program. You note that a love scene is playing and you see that the camera is caressing the bare skin of the two lovers on the screen. They move slowly caressing one another.

Their faces are obscured but you can tell that they both are enjoying the encounter and you feel yourself respond to what you are seeing. The woman raises her arm and exposes her breast and you note that the man's nipple is hard and his breathing rapid. They turn towards the camera and you see their faces for the first time, the man has Down's syndrome and the woman has microcephaly. They kiss, she parts her lips and his tongue finds her lips and then they press one into the other.

As you read the scene above how did you react to the discovery that the two people were not only developmentally disabled but also were visibly handicapped? The description of the kiss that followed the disclosure of their disability ... how did you react to this? Now a little further, imagine the loving scene above and place it into a group home or apartment program of an agency for the developmentally handicapped. What is going to happen to them if they are caught? What would you do if you were doing the 'catching?' Should they be allowed to continue their relationship? What if the people on the screen were two women? Two men? Would that make a difference?

As you answer these questions think more personally about yourself. How comfortable are you with being you? Have you made peace with your sexuality, attractiveness, relationships? If you are going to expect yourself to be able to deal honestly and maturely with the sexuality of others, you need to deal honestly with yourself. Each person carries monogrammed emotional baggage that affects their decisions, their actions and their opinions. You need to be aware of your own.

It is totally unethical for you to let personal discomfort splash over onto the lives of even a single person with a disability in your care.

• Unlock the prison door. Don't look at the prison of protection as a theoretical model. Go back to the page that has the line drawing of the person in the prison. Mentally give the name of a person with a disability to whom you provide service to the line drawing. Now ask yourself questions. Has this person been denied sex education? Why? Has this person ever had the opportunity to learn how to make decisions? How can you start teaching? Has this person been locked away from society? What has that done to them? Has this person been punished for loving another? Do they understand that love is a good thing?

After answering the questions, begin to look at what you need to teach that person. Remember whenever you read a book or hear a speaker, take the information and say "How does this apply to Sandy?" This is the only place to start.

• Honour your expertise and expect respect. Please don't think that you need to have some kind of degree to be an expert. Any front line staff that I have met who has worked with a person for more than a couple of months has greater expertise in an individual than any 'expert' or 'consultant.' If you are front line you need to learn that you deserve respect, that your clients deserve respect, and make sure that systems and agencies act accordingly.

Yesterday, I gave a workshop in the United States and at the end took questions. A man asked me how he could make someone who had never felt good about themselves into someone who honoured themselves. This was a difficult question and before I could answer a young woman stood up and said, "I think I know." I asked her to go ahead. She said that she thought that part of how people learn about themselves is from how others treat them. If we treat people as if they have value then they will learn to see themselves as having value. If we treat them as if they are hopelessly incompetent then they will see themselves as hopelessly incompetent.

She then went on to say that there was a major flaw with the golden rule. For those who didn't understand her reference to mineral morality she quoted it, "Do unto others as you would have them do unto you." She said that the problem was most people let other people do horrible things to them daily and have become so used to unkindness that they expect it. She ended by saying that if we are to be expected to treat our clients with respect, then the agencies need to begin treating their staff with respect.

She sat down to more resounding applause than I ever got. Or earned.

## SUMMARY

As AIDS took its toll on the Gay community one began to hear more and more urgent defiant demands for change. This level of commitment was remarkable as they had to deal with those who said that "AIDS was God's punishment." Gay men and lesbian women didn't retreat in light of vicious attacks from those who see God as someone who is tyrannical, cruel and childish in the use of power. The urgency of civil liberties becomes so much more compelling when faced with loss of ability and loss of life. One slogan I read has stayed with me since I first saw it simply printed in white on a black banner:

## THE CLOSET IS NO PLACE TO DIE
Amen! To this let us add:

A PRISON IS NO PLACE FOR THE INNOCENT TO LIVE

# 3

# *Thank the Goddess for Feminists*

Room service. Don't those two words sound like they were meant for each other? Well in fact, room service can get a little tedious. I had been travelling for several weeks and arrived on a Sunday afternoon in Terrace, B.C. Now Terrace is not often in your holiday travel plans but it is a very pretty city. After dropping my luggage just inside the door I fell on the bed. Tired but hungry. I automatically reached for the room service menu. Now the hotel was nice but the menu was a variety of foods fried in a variety of greases. Great, that means I am going to have to go out and forage for food.

A couple of hours later, I bundled up against Terrace's first winter blast and was standing on the street. Where now? Well, to my right were a number of young teens and pre-teens hanging outside a video arcade. That means of course, go left. No large person freely walks past this age group. Adolescent hormones do not a sensitive person make. In fact I've always thought that a mother's right to choose should be extended through the teen years.

Going left I walked past several darkened windows and was nearing a Chinese restaurant. I love Chinese food. Especially on the road. I approached and entered. I had a choice of cafe to my left or restaurant to my right. I noticed a group of late-teens in a booth in the cafe. That means of course, go right. I entered the restaurant.

I found a table in the far corner and sat with my back against the wall, a primitive human behaviour equivalent to dogs turning around three times before lying down. There were two other peopled tables, four people at each, both of which stopped talking upon my entry and their heads swivelled towards me. Blatant staring is acceptable practice in small towns. I was given the once over twice and then they eventually found their chow mein more interesting than my girth and they returned to their plates.

The waitress who served me was a large woman with the most incredible blond hair I have ever seen. I mean this hair was YEL-LOW. Crayon yellow. She wore it like a helmet and she walked with authority. Any man who told her a blond joke would soon find a part of his anatomy stretched and tied into an interesting bow around his neck. You didn't fool with her. I ordered, meekly, the combo dinner for 1,B. She didn't write it down. I'm sure here hair wouldn't let a memory slip out!

I had brought with me a card to send home. When I'm on the road I get very lonely. Having dinner alone can be bad enough in the room where one has the television for company. But alone and out is awful. In a restaurant you leave yourself open for pity from other tables. So I take a card and write a letter home over dinner and then mail it on the way back to the hotel. This way I get to have what I like best, food and a one way conversation with the person I love. I am, of course, less alone.

The food arrived with a genteel 'plunk' on the table. I was told to enjoy the food. It wasn't a request. The food was passable and during my repast I worked on the card. It is hard to be far from home and to communicate. It is like two people who want to use words like, love, missing, longing and sadness but are afraid that if they do it might increase the pain of separation, not ease it. This is probably an error but one I repeat often.

During the meal, about midpoint two Native Canadian women entered the restaurant. They stood for a moment, looking a little lost and confused, one noticed the "please seat yourself" sign stapled to the wall and they both moved into the restaurant. Neither spoke. In fact, neither even looked at each other. They sat down at the table nearest me. One, the younger looking sat with her back to me. She sat her large oversized purse down with finality. I couldn't wait to see her and blondie in discourse. But I was wrong, the waitress brought them their menus and for a moment when the waitress was passing a menu across the woman near me, her hand rested gently on her shoulder. A squeeze and it was gone.

I could not help but notice the two women. Firstly, they were my closest neighbours in the restaurant, secondly they were behaving oddly. They looked uncomfortable with one another. They looked like two strangers out for dinner. You can tell when friends are out with friends, their movements and gestures fit together somehow. There is a symmetry as elegant as ballet when you watch the body language of two people who love each other and know each other well. The dance of friendship was not there in their movements. They were oddly matched, one would start and then stop. Abrupt and jerky inter-relations. Why were they together?

They did not speak for a long time. They buried themselves in the menu and did not surface until decisions had been made. They did not, as friends do, order two or three dishes to share. Instead they each ordered a different dinner for one. The blond waitress took the order but did not leave right away she stood and talked. It was obvious that she knew the one with the large purse well. She joked with them and when she left they were talking to one another.

I looked at her differently now, this waitress. I had classified her into that little box we put people in when we use superiority and prejudice as the glass in the spectacles with which we view people. She was a better therapist than I. She was able to assess the situation and rather than sit down and help them through the situation, she merely facilitated the talking. This blonde-helmeted woman had a large body, she needed one to make room for her heart.

Even though they were now talking the one farthest from me seemed unable to concentrate even on the most mundane of conversations. Every time the door opened she was like a doe in the woods. She would be fully alive, fully alert, fully aware. Then seeing who entered she would relax and breath easier. After food had been ordered and was being consumed she began to cry.

She turned to her friend and told her quietly and painfully about her life for the last twenty-two years. She described incredible physical and sexual abuse by her husband. She did not detail the abuse and hearing such pain and cruelty explained unencumbered by needless words was hard to listen to. Like her table mate I too had stopped eating and just sat and listened to her story.

She talked about her wedding day. She had been so happy that day. She was eighteen and about to leave a father who had hurt her. She was escaping. A beautiful calm came over her face as she remembered that day. Turning to her friend she said, "You looked so beautiful that day, you were my maid of honor. I was so happy." The calm that had graced her face did not stay. She remembered her honeymoon, it was on that trip that she was first beaten by her husband. "He told me that I couldn't see my friends any more. He told me that his friends were now my friends. He told me that if I didn't obey him I would be sorry. I stuck up to him, I told him that you and I had been best friends since we were girls and we would be friends for the rest of our lives. He put me in the hospital."

"When we came back, I knew I couldn't see you. Not so much because I was afraid of him for me. He told me he would hurt you too. I couldn't put you in danger. I never called you again. If I saw you on the street, I went the other way. I knew I was hurting you, I just hoped you understood." She stopped and looked at her friend. "After twenty-two years, we are old women now. I call you and you still come out with me. When I left him yesterday, I had no one of my own. I could only think of you. And you came. I can't believe that you came with me." She was crying hard, but still silently. No one in the restaurant seemed to notice.

Then I realized that she would have had to learn to grieve and weep in silence or she would have probably been punished even more severely. Even now you would have had to look directly at her to realize that she was talking about anything more serious than the weather. Who was this man, and what right did he have to do this to a woman who loved him? A woman who had trusted him to take her away from abuse. I hated him.

"I need to talk about something else. Can we talk about things like we did as girls, can we do that?" Her friend tried, talking about her life and things that had happened to her. Simple everyday things and as she spoke the tears dried in her friend's eyes. Even so, they did not converse as friends converse, it was stilted and it was awkward. Anger tinged her voice when the beaten one next spoke, "I *HATE* him for this. He took this away from me, he took my ability to talk with you away from me. And I know you hate me. I know you came here tonight but I know deep down you hate me for abandoning you. I know that you think I did it on purpose. I know that you think I should have left him a long time ago. I know you hate me."

During this short emotional speech the woman with the large bag reached down into her bag and pulled from it a stack of large square white envelopes some quite yellowed with age. She set them down on the table in front of her and then turned to her friend and lifted her hand and stroked dry a place where tears had left tracks. "No, I never hated you but I did miss you." She then passed over the stack of envelopes to her friend, "There are twenty-two there."

"What are they?"

"Birthday cards. I bought you one each year. I didn't send them, I knew he would hurt you. I kept them. I just hoped that we could be friends again. Of course I came tonight, one does not love and just let it go."

A sob burst out in the restaurant, but it came from my table. The two women turned to look at me and the table of four that had watched me enter turned and the blond waitress turned. I was mortified, I knew there would be three interpretations of my behaviour in that restaurant. To the women on my right, they knew I had sat listening to them, to the others in the restaurant, I was a pitiable person crying alone at a table, to the blond waitress I was a man who also understood pain like she must have.

Getting myself under control, I began eating again just to finish my food. The women to my right, now aware of being overheard turned to lighter conversation and did much better. I glanced again and saw that they now fed themselves off both plates, sharing food as friends. Just before finishing a young couple came into the restaurant. The smaller tables were now all filled and they were invited by the waitress to sit at a large table for six. They were clearly dating and were enjoying being out with each other.

After seating them the waitress came and gave them their menus. When she turned to leave the man reached across the table and took the menu from the woman, she looked confused at first and then let it be taken from her. He then studied the menu, I waited for him to ask her what she liked or wanted, he didn't. When the waitress returned he ordered the dinner for two C and an order of their special chow mein. The waitress left and the woman leaned over and asked, "What's the special chow mein?" and he responded in a witty testosterone kind of way, "It's special chow mein." And she laughed.

At that point I wanted to get up and go over to that table. I wanted to take that young woman by her arm and escort her over to the table to my right. I wanted to tell her to talk with them for just a couple of minutes. I wanted to, but I didn't. I finished, paid my bill and left. I returned to my room and sat in the still and quiet of a Sunday night in downtown Terrace and I cried. Both for the courage of the woman rediscovering her power and reconnecting with friendship and for the woman whose power was already slipping from her.

## PLAIN LANGUAGE

- Once you give up your power it is a struggle to get it back.

- Those that take your power will invariably use it to hurt you.

### *WHAT YOU CAN DO*

- Never Ever Ever Give Up Your Power. Do not confuse loving someone with losing yourself. Whoever you are, man or woman, love can make you feel that you want to give over everything to someone else. Those who love you will accept your sentiment but refuse the gift of your power. I have learned that those who love me do not want to control me. Those who love me, love ME.

- Never Ever Ever Take Someone Else's Power. It is difficult enough living your own life without having to do it for someone else. To say that power corrupts is incorrect. People who explore and discover their own power as individuals are not corrupted by the knowledge. It is the quest for power over others that begins the corruption and the gaining of it that corrodes your soul.

(Did those two last sections sound exactly the same? They were. I have learned that it's not just people with disabilities that have to have some messages given over and over and over and ... well you get the idea.)

## THANK THE GENDER-FREE DEITY, INDEED

Before beginning to discuss an approach to preventing the sexual assault of people with developmental disabilities, it is important to stop and say "Thanks." It is my firm belief that if the women's movement had not raised the issue of sexual victimization and fought for society to recognize this evil we would not now be addressing the issue. The story above shows how women have been conditioned to accept what men give them. Two women separated by twenty years' time, one gave up power to men another is about to do the same. This must stop.

An analysis of sexual victimization is an analysis of power. Thus far in the book we have focused on how we imprison people because of their victimization or perceived vulnerability. Some of you might think that I am exaggerating to make a point. I am not, however, even slightly embroidering the facts. In fact, I go further to state that the situations that I have outlined for people with disabilities are exactly parallel to those that have occurred for women. Let's look at what we have done to women.

• We have stated that women are vulnerable because of their gender. We have made vulnerability a character trait of women.

• We acknowledge that gender is immutable.

• Since women are vulnerable because of who they are, they need protection. And since their gender is not going to change, they are going to have to alter their movements.

• Women should not go out at night. They are vulnerable people who need protection from the dark.

• Women should not wear particular clothing. They are vulnerable people who need protection from their own attractiveness.

41

• Women should not work at particular jobs. They are vulnerable people who need to be protected from a full range of employment options.

• Women should not go into a bar alone. They are vulnerable people who need to be protected from a full range of social options.

• Women should not make their own decisions. They are vulnerable people who need to be protected by those stronger, wiser and more - well - masculine.

• Women should not be given sex education that casts themselves as sexual equals to men. They are vulnerable people who need to be protected from sexual knowledge.

• Women are vulnerable. They are just naturally weaker and inferior to men.

Everything said above is FALSE. Yet it has been said. More than having been said, it is held to be true. The women's movement has finally said, "Enough!" Anyone who has not been to a "Take Back the Night" march should go. These marches are held by the women's community. It is their way of saying that it is no longer an acceptable solution to cage the victim. Women gather in large numbers and march through a neighbourhood where a rapist has been preying. The march signals a breaking of all the rules. They march at night. They march proud. They march as free citizens. They march with power.

The march, in symbol and in fact, flouts the past approach of imprisoning the innocent. The march essentially says:

IT IS NO LONGER AN ACCEPTABLE SOLUTION TO GET WOMEN OFF THE STREETS AT NIGHT — THE ONLY ACCEPTABLE SOLUTION IS TO GET THE RAPIST OFF THE STREETS AT NIGHT.

If we adopted the same strategy, that of saying "ENOUGH!" No more pain and hurt of people with disabilities, this would be the beginning. But judging by the places where people with disabilities are abused we would need to have "Take Back the Group Home, the Special Buses, the Workshop" marches.

IT IS NO LONGER AN ACCEPTABLE SOLUTION TO BLAME PEOPLE WITH DISABILITIES FOR BEING VICTIM-IZED — THE ONLY ACCEPTABLE SOLUTION IS TO BLAME THE VICTIMIZER. AND GET RID OF THEM.

## SUMMARY

Oddly we have been acting as if there is rape because there are women rather than realizing that there is rape because there are rapists. Women want a few simple facts acknowledged. Children are not molested because they are children. Women are not raped because they are women. People with disabilities are not abused because they have a disability.

*   *   *

Molestation happens because of molesters.

Rape happens because of rapists.

Abuse happens because of abusers.

# 4

# *LOOK UP*

I was at a conference. I was there to do a presentation on the Ring of Safety. As I was setting up and trying to prepare myself for giving the lecture a young man approached me. He was in a state of agitation that could only be described as a combination of desperation and dread. He wanted to talk with me. I could see that whatever he had to say was very big and I had very little time. I asked him if we could talk at break and he agreed. Expecting to see him sit down in the room, I was surprised to see him leave the room taking a chair so that he could sit outside the room during the first part of the lecture. I had to put him out of my mind. I am a nervous lecturer and have to deal with my own significant insecurities before I have the courage to face a crowd. The room filled and I began.

At first break he returned on cue. I noticed blood on his hand. He had chewed the cuticles down past the quick. He was hurting himself. This was going to be more than a fifteen minute conversation. I told him that I had a two hour wait at the airport after my lecture and before my flight. Did he have a car and would he drive me to the airport? Then we would have both time and privacy.

We got in his car and momentarily I worried that I may be placing myself in danger. What did I know of him? But my fear was unfounded, he was a gentle kind man in distress. He told me that he had begun teaching sex education because of reading my book "I Contact" and had come to really enjoy the role of both teacher and counsellor with the individuals that attended his class. His agency wanted to share his resource and create greater social opportunities for their clients so he began teaching the course in a night school setting wherein people with disabilities coming from a variety of settings could attend. The class was very popular.

All this was wonderful but his voice was filled with regret for having undertaken this responsibility. He told me that in one of the sessions during his last series of classes, a young woman with a disability reported that she was presently being sexually abused by one of the male staff in her group home. He was taken aback by the revelation and asked to speak to her afterwards. He got details and immediately called the director of the agency to inform her of what had happened in the class. The director assured him that the victimization was not possible. She personally knew the staff involved and was sure that he would never do anything like that. Even so he pressed on stating that he had believed the report. He was assured that an investigation would take place.

The next class was two weeks later. He said that he was disappointed that the young woman was not in his class. After class he called her group home to see if she was sick. He was told in a brusque officious tone of voice that this young woman had accidentally drowned in the bathtub days before. Tears ran down his face. He did not sob. He did not moan. He simply cried. I knew that these tears were flowing down his face following the flow of many before. He was scared. He thought maybe he killed her.

Did I think he was responsible for her death? This is what he asked me.

No. Of course not. The only person responsible for a crime is the person who commits it. I will say however, that we need to ensure that we not only report an allegation but that we make sure the person is protected from their abuser. Remember abusers, almost to a one, say "If you talk, I'll kill." They mean it. These are not nice people. If they know that abuse will damage the soul of their victim yet they proceed, doesn't it make sense that they don't care about the body either?

## PLAIN LANGUAGE

- Victimizers are dangerous.

- Proceed carefully, having thought out all angles.

46

• Please be careful. In zeal to find sexual assault we can rush too fast and be unprepared for what we find. Never approach the issue of sexual victimization of people with disabilities without much forethought. If you suspect after reading this chapter that someone you work with has been abused, please do not rush to them and assault them with questions. You need to have advice from your agency. Find out what the policy is in your agency, province, state for reporting sexual victimization. Find out how your agency plans to protect a person who has been victimized from their abuser during the investigation. If there is no policy, create a task force. This is a life and death issue.

• Look Up. I have two dogs. Fred and Eric by name. Fred was planned, Eric was an accident. Eric, the youngest, was found abandoned in the parking lot of a large mall. I made the mistake of picking him up. He relaxed his little puppy body into my arms and then set about charming me by nuzzling his nose into my neck. Eric came home and joined the family. Fred was just a little less than jubilant at the arrival of a new pup. The first couple of days they spent apart from one another surveying each other. Then on a sunny day we went down to a cleared field not far from the house. This was and is Fred's favourite spot. Here he can run! He is a beautiful dog and seeing him in full flight is extraordinary.

Eric was not up for running like Fred. After all his chubby little puppy legs couldn't carry him that fast. But soon they were romping together. Then an intruder. A squirrel appeared on the field. In Fred's doggie mind, squirrels are not living beings. They are rawhide bones come to life. He was in hot pursuit. He ran quickly and silently, the squirrel almost literally took off. Eric stumbled behind. When Eric tripped and crashed down, Fred momentarily took his eyes of the squirrel and glanced back to see what caused the noise. Seeing Eric squashed against the ground, I'm convinced I saw a look of sheer pleasure on Fred's face. He resumed the chase.

But the squirrel was gone. Fred couldn't see him anywhere. In fact, the squirrel had taken the opportunity to escape and had jumped a jump that even Elvis Stoyko would be proud of and landed on a branch just out of Fred's line of vision. Trusting his nose, not his eyes, Fred began to trace the squirrel's scent on the ground. He ran to the left. To the right. Back to the left. Eric thought this all great fun and kept trying to jump on Fred. Try as I might to avoid the comparison, they kind of reminded me of Wally and the Beaver. Fred was at a loss. The scent just seemed to stop. Eventually he just gave up and trotted back to us wanting one of the treats I carry in my pocket. He munched on the treat trying to forget the squirrel that was sitting without moving on a branch in clear sight. If he had just looked up and seen what was in front of him.

Fred reminded me of myself at work. I can have a goal. A clear purpose and in a moment's distraction I can lose sight of what I'm doing. I end up, nose down searching for clues and evidence of what I seek. As such I spend most of my days looking everywhere but where I should. I need to learn to "Look Up" and see what's in front of me. As a matter of fact, on the upper right hand corner of my computer screen I have the words, "Dave, Look Up" on a yellow sticky as a reminder that we as people and me as an individual have trouble seeing what's directly in front of our faces. I suggest that you too, need to learn to "Look Up" and if you are anything like me, you will need to remind yourself constantly.

• Become familiar with signs of abuse. I am about to present to you the signs of abuse. But I do so with hesitation. I'm afraid that one of two things will happen. The first is kind of the same as the "med student's syndrome." We have all heard of young doctors reading about a disease or syndrome and automatically diagnosing themselves with the illness. The same phenomenon can happen here. The list of behaviours that are possible indices of abuse are so general that as a reader you may be thinking, "My Gosh, Helen has trouble sleeping. She must have been abused." This is a dangerous assumption to make. Remember that these have been documented as concerns but that the list isn't constructed in such a way that you are supposed to determine that someone has been a victim of abuse just because they exhibit a number of these behaviours. The second is that a person with a disability will be communicating to you in a way different than anyone has ever documented. By limiting yourself to lists and research you can miss the individual who is communicating the abuse in different ways. Remember a cardinal rule - any change that comes out of the blue needs to be investigated.

*   *   *

## SEXISM IS SEXISM - AVOID IT AT ALL COSTS

A young woman with a disability had been sexually assaulting one of the men in her residence. She was much brighter than he and had developed a pattern of offense that allowed her to proceed for a long time. He had no verbal skills and even though his behaviour changed as a result of the assaults no one noticed, or if they did, they didn't ask all the questions that would have led them to discover his victimization. Finally, someone noticed that he had bruising on both sides of his chest.

What was found during an investigation was that the victimizer would go into his room at night, pull down his pyjamas and fellate him until he got an erection. Because the erection would not last, she would jump on him to get his penis inside her while it was still stiff. She had become more careless and had to be quicker each time. As a result she would land with her knees digging hard into his sides.

This is an ugly scene. When his victimization was discussed at a team meeting one of the female staff, noted for her sense of humour, made a joke of it. She suggested that now that he was having sex it was time they taught him to smoke. People laughed.

## PLAIN LANGUAGE

• Victims can be young, old, fat, thin, pretty, plain, handsome, ordinary, women, men.

• Victimizers can be old, young, thin, fat, plain, pretty, ordinary, handsome, men, women.

*   *   *

# BEHAVIOURAL INDICES OF SEXUAL ABUSE

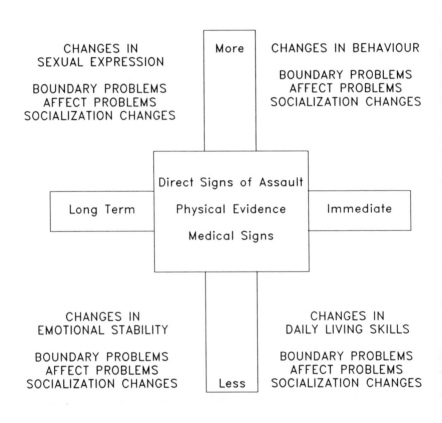

CHANGES IN
SEXUAL EXPRESSION

BOUNDARY PROBLEMS
AFFECT PROBLEMS
SOCIALIZATION CHANGES

More

CHANGES IN BEHAVIOUR

BOUNDARY PROBLEMS
AFFECT PROBLEMS
SOCIALIZATION CHANGES

Long Term

Direct Signs of Assault

Physical Evidence

Medical Signs

Immediate

CHANGES IN
EMOTIONAL STABILITY

BOUNDARY PROBLEMS
AFFECT PROBLEMS
SOCIALIZATION CHANGES

Less

CHANGES IN
DAILY LIVING SKILLS

BOUNDARY PROBLEMS
AFFECT PROBLEMS
SOCIALIZATION CHANGES

Over the past several years I have been conducting workshops on sexual victimization for staff who work with people with disabilities. I have asked them to list the behaviours that they have seen in clients they *knew* to have been sexually assaulted. I have gone through the lists and it is probably best to understand the behavioural changes by looking at the diagram provided.

CAUTION: As you read the list be aware that when something is listed this means that a *change* has happened. For example, someone used to have no difficulty sleeping, now has a difficulty. If you have only a limited history with the people you serve and you wonder if their behaviour is a possible indicator of past abuse then the only thing you can do is to carefully review their file. If you note that they didn't have trouble sleeping until age fourteen when they were first put on sleeping medication then you have cause for concern. Even so, the existence of these behaviours in any of your clients does not mean that they necessarily have been abused.

DIRECT SIGNS OF ASSAULT: Physical Evidence

In the center of the diagram you see that there are direct signs of assault. I first thought that it would be unnecessary to list these in a book on assault because it seemed so obvious that people would see that if there were actually physical evidence of wounding, questions would be asked. Jeffrey Dalhmer's case dissuaded me of this belief. Remember that a young boy escaped from Dalhmer's apartment and even though there was direct evidence that he had been hurt, the police returned him to the apartment. As such, I no longer believe that people see what is in front of their faces. I believe that we are all, like Fred, too busy with our nose to the ground to notice what is happening right in front of us.

- Difficulty in walking or sitting.

- Torn or bloody underclothing.

- Bruises or bleeding in the genital or anal area.

- Pain or itching in the genital area.

51

It would be beneficial for you to have a workshop provided for you by your local police or rape crisis center. Ask them to do a workshop on sexual abuse and how to deal with evidence. They will best be able to advise you.

DIRECT SIGNS OF ASSAULT: Medical Signs

There are the obvious:

- Pregnancy

- Venereal disease

And the less obvious:

- Ulcers: Living with abuse or with an abuser is a stressful existence that takes a physical toll.

- Unexplained stomach aches: People with disabilities who have not had the benefit of sex education may have difficulty reporting abuse because of a lack of vocabulary. Most have had general education about their bodies and therefore know arms, legs, eyes, nose and other non-sexual parts. Some have attempted to report sexual abuse by naming the organ that is closest to their genitals that they can name. Hence, unexplained stomach complaints.

The Quadrants

You will notice that the diagram has four quadrants separated by two lines. The horizontal line represents the speed at which the change is seen. Some changes are more immediate and others are more long term and develop over time. The vertical line represents a quantitative change. Some behaviours increase and others decrease. (Again, these are general trends that have been reported to me. It may be vastly different with an individual you know.) The four main headings reflect the areas that people are often referred for service as a result of their behaviours after an assault has occurred. These areas are Changes in Behaviour, Changes in Daily Living

Skills, Changes in Emotional Stability and Changes in Sexual Expression.

In looking at the feedback sheets from my audiences it seems that the lists of behaviours that I have been given can be further categorized into three basic categories of problems that evidence themselves as behaviour after a sexual assault. Boundary-problems which break down into either a deterioration of boundaries or an aggressive assertion of boundaries. Affect problems which result from a person's distress from the assault getting in the way of their ability to control their affect or as a means of provoking affect in others. The final category is Socialization changes in which the person's social skills or socialization patterns are altered after the assault.

**CHANGES IN BEHAVIOUR** (Usually Quick and Usually an Increase)

Boundaries-Related

- aggression: This aggression is usually related to someone entering into a client's personal boundaries. Staff may attempt to touch for routine assistance and be struck. This is approach related aggression and is not tied to any type of demand.

- non-compliance: This is usually related to a refusal to do activities that involve personal space. Refusal to shower, shave, wash hands, or change clothes.

These two behaviours are often seen to increase when an individual is assertively attempting to establish or defend boundaries. As theses two categories of behaviour are often seen as problematic, it is important to note that they occur as a result of a need to protect personal or physical space. Agencies should be cautious not to program a person out of a behaviour that has been developed to protect oneself.

- accident proneness: This is a result of a person rushing through commands to finish and be out of sight of staff. Clients may look like they have impulse control problems but in reality it is a combination of rush and anxiety that causes the accidents.

- increased time spent asleep: Again this is a boundary issue. These are individuals who are building safety around them by opting to sleep rather than be in interaction with others.

## Affect-Related

- self-injury: Unlike most self-injury, this seems to be a form of self punishment. Many people reported self-injury as an indicator of past sexual abuse and those who described it usually described face slapping, hand slapping or genital slapping. This may be better described as self punishment rather than self-injury.

- temper control: When a person has not had previous difficulty with managing their temper, it should be seen as significant that they are no longer successfully managing routine stressors.

- impulse control: Like temper control, people who are acting on impulse rather than thinking things through, it is usually because of some distracting thoughts or feelings. Staff need to know what is causing the problem before trying to fix it.

## Changes in Socialization Patterns

- phobic compliance: When individuals seem not only overly compliant (which is a common problem for most people with disabilities) but have an edge of fear in their willingness to please, this may be an indicator that they are living with fear.

- distractibility: Difficulty in getting an individual to attend to task. Very highly distractible, attempts to socialize and converse but cannot. Concentration is gone.

- increased eating: Often recorded as a huge appetite increase. Clients who would normally eat a balanced meal are now eating more at social times or times when they are in company with others. Sneak eating may also occur.

\*   \*   \*

**CHANGES IN LIVING SKILLS** (Usually Quick and Usually a Decrease)

Boundary-Related

Skill loss (discriminating privacy)

- privacy violations: A loss of a sense of personal modesty. Walking naked from the bedroom or bathroom, wearing underclothes over top of clothing, masturbating in public places are all privacy violations.

- violating others' privacy rules: Touching other people inappropriately. This is seen here as a result of a desensitization of the person to what their touch means. They seem to no longer discriminate other people's bodies as being private.

- violating other people's property: A loss of understanding of other people's possessions as belonging to them. They simply take whatever they want without regard to someone else's reaction.

Affect Related

- skill loss (performance deterioration): It is important to note how people with disabilities learn. If you watch a person with a disability who has learned a functional skill like, say, shoe-tying you will notice a slight difference in how they perform the skill than how you do the same thing. People with disabilities often take longer to learn and as such are taught using a task analysis. A task analysis breaks a skill into its component parts and works a person through a task from start to completion. For many people with disabilities these skills do not become rote. Instead, when watching them you will see them concentrate on what they are doing and take themselves through the task analysis.

When a person with a disability is living with stress there may be an inability to concentrate on routine tasks. As a result the person loses skills. Often care providers may mistake a loss of skills to a person's inability to retain when in fact the issue is a loss of concentration.

Changes in Socialization Patterns

- skill loss (Social Skills Deterioration): Loss of manners and other niceties when in a social situation. Loss of eating skills, spilling food and other behaviours that may serve the purpose of being sent out of the social situation.

*   *   *

**CHANGES IN EMOTIONAL STABILITY** (Usually Slow and Usually Less)

Boundary-Related

- touch phobia: Intense dislike of being touched and touching others. Discomfort may show itself as aggression (see Behavioural section)

- discomfort with eye contact: Doesn't want to be looked at. May hide away in odd places. Can be mistaken for non-compliance but is a means of getting out of public view.

- difficulty sleeping: People who don't feel safe in an environment may react by being unable to go to sleep. Anxiety is perhaps one of the greatest sleep interruptors for me! These individuals have been reported in the questionnaires as fighting the sleep medications that they are given. These people are trying to protect themselves in their environment and they see vigilance as their best tool for keeping safe. There are two important things to note here:

• there may be a connection between "difficulty sleeping" in this section and "increased time spent asleep." More than one person noted that they found that the individual would have difficulty sleeping at home yet arrive at work and sleep. In these cases home was unsafe and work was safe so the person was able to slip into sleep at the day programme.

• nightmares may be a factor in the difficulty sleeping. The person may fear sleep because of night terrors or because of the dreams that they have.

Affect Related

- loss of affect: The individual exhibits a flat affect in most situations. No longer expresses joy or pleasure.

- loss of appetite: Develops finicky eating habits. May develop into anorexia nervosa.

- depression and suicide: The most often cited indicator of sexual assault in the questionnaires was depression. A few people stated that their clients talked about death or suicide, no-one was aware of a situation where a person with a disability committed suicide as a result of an abusive situation. This is not to say it has not or could not occur, only that no-one reported a suicide on a very unscientific questionnaire.

Change in Socialization Patterns

- avoidance of former close friends and a fear of formerly trusted staff: People who have been victimized may avoid people they trust for a number of reasons; let's list just five:

1) They see the person they trust in contact with their abuser and they don't know how to judge loyalties.

2) They are attempting to protect their friends from their abuser so they avoid them.

3) They fear judgement and blame.

4) They think that everyone knows and no one wants to help.

5) They fear their own resolve and think that if they spend time with someone they trust they may accidentally tell. They fear that their abuser will make good on his threat to kill them.

- change in leisure habits: When a person suddenly decides that they dislike an activity that has always given them pleasure in the past.

*   *   *

**CHANGE IN SEXUAL EXPRESSION** (Usually Slow and Usually More)

Boundary-related:

- sophisticated sexual behaviour: This is particularly true for children with disabilities in that they demonstrate sexual behaviour that is more sophisticated than mere sexual curiosity or sexual play. These are often performed in public places or involve the violation of another person's boundaries.

- unusual sexual behaviour: A sudden appearance of sexual behaviour that is out of the norm. Inserting objects in vagina or anus, masturbating constantly through clothing. Again the person doesn't discriminate time or place.

- talking about sexual issues in highly public places: When this occurs it may be due to a loss of boundaries (See Change in Living Skills section) but may also be due to the fact that the person chooses a place that they define as safe (i.e. Mc Donald's with a lot of people around) to bring up the subject of sexuality. The security of people around and the comfortable atmosphere may make highly public places seem 'safer' than private places that they have learned to define as 'unsafe.' (i.e. private bedroom with staff).

- sexually assaultive behaviour: Most individuals that have been served through the Sex Offender Treatment program have been sexually abused themselves.

Affect related

- fear reaction to sex education materials: Sex education materials often provoke anxiety, this means that the anxiety goes beyond what is typical and becomes almost phobic.

Changes in Socialization Patterns

- makes false accusations: Instead of naming a perpetrator who is feared, the individual may name someone that they feel is safe and will not hurt them. This is very damaging and the client is often unprepared for the fallout.

- sexualizes non-sexual social cues: The individual may see everything that is done as sexual. A hug becomes sexualized and the individual believes that everyone wants to fondle them.

## SUMMARY

It cannot be stated often enough that a person may not have been abused even if they show a number of the behaviours above. You may then well ask the question, "If they aren't definite, then why make up a list at all?" The answer is simply that the list is aimed at sensitizing you and other clinicians to be aware that the behaviours that they see may be communicating that the individual is being abused. Every person who works with a disability needs to learn to ask questions about their clients' safety as a routine part of their day. This does a number of things, first it makes it more likely that you will catch abuse should it occur, and second it may prevent abuse in that your vigilance and awareness will create a hostile environment for abusers.

The other reason to consider this list is that, if it is true as it seems to be, that sexual abuse of people with disabilities shows itself quickly in relatively superficial ways (Behavioural Problems and Skill Deficits) then dealing with the problem right away might avoid some of the more long term problems that lead to incarceration (sexual violation of others) or psychiatric problems (depression and suicide). Remember .....

LOOK UP

# 5

# THE RING OF SAFETY

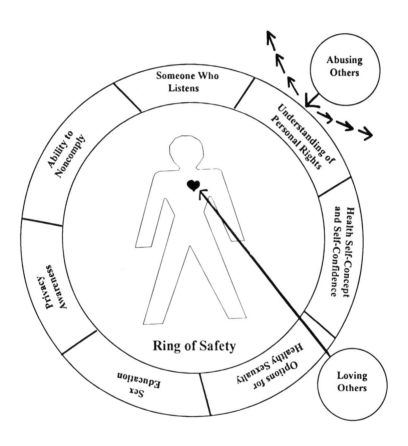

Someone Who Listens

Ability to Noncomply

Privacy Awareness

Sex Education

Options for Healthy Sexuality

Health Self-Concept and Self-Confidence

Understanding of Personal Rights

Abusing Others

Loving Others

Ring of Safety

The Ring of Safety brings together the skills that will increase a person with a developmental disability's ability to protect themselves. This model is entirely different from the Prison of Protection for two reasons. First, the person with the developmental disability is seen as capable of being their own first line of defense. Second, it places the responsibility on the shoulders of the victimizer rather than because of a characteristic, on the shoulders of the victim. This model is clearly feminist, the "Prison" model is clearly paternalistic.

Let's look at each of the components:

## OPPORTUNITY FOR HEALTHY SEXUALITY

Main Message: FREEDOM IS GOOD

We were called in to consult with an agency that was having difficulty with one of their male clients who had developed an "addiction" to phone sex. Somehow he had discovered that you could call a number and a friendly, no ... very, VERY friendly woman would talk nice, no ... very, VERY nice to him. The agency was hit with a phone bill that was in the hundreds of dollars. Let's face it, a man who works at a sheltered industry can hardly afford a quarter for a pay phone so a phone bill in the hundreds is difficult. Imagine you personally trying to pay off the national debt. Sorry that's too extreme an example, you and I work in social services, imagine trying to meet your mortgage monthly. There was a moral crisis, precipitated of course by a financial crisis.

I met with him and found that he was using the phone calls as a means of meeting sexual needs. (I got that right away because I have both a degree and a penis. In fact, I have two framed degrees on display so we can accurately say that my walls are much better hung than I am.) In talking with him he stated that he had trouble masturbating because it was hard to concentrate long enough, the phone calls helped him to focus. Knowing the importance of fantasy in sexuality and knowing that phone sex lines can sometimes feed into deviant fantasies, we suggested that some tape recorded fantasies would do the trick. (I can't help it, it's late, I've been writing all day.) The tapes were made and delivered. I was done.

Until the next month. The bill was even higher. So was the volume of the discussion about his behaviour in his apartment. A block was placed on the line to stop these calls from occurring. We gave him some more tapes so he would have variety and felt that now that the option of the interactive sex talk was not available to him he would opt instead for the prerecorded fantasy tapes. Wrong.

The following month it was discovered that he had gone into empty offices at the sheltered industry and used instructors' phones to call the phone sex line. The bill for sex calls was smaller but they were coming from employee offices. People were not pleased. I was to try again.

I was confused because he had the tapes and surely could use them. In fact, he said that he did use them and they did help him to become aroused. So why the phone calls? I decided to gather information on just what happened on the call.

## WARNING ** GRAPHIC SEXUAL MATERIAL **

(I'm not kidding)

I asked him to tell me what happened on the call. He was shy but willing to tell me about his calls to Kristie (with a heart used to dot the last i). So this woman had a name. One name and probably a hundred voices, I thought, but asked him to press on and tell me about the call.

"Well, I call and we say, Hi."

"Yes, then what?" Calm, clinical, I'm good.

"She tells me that she has really, really, REALLY big tits."

"Uh huh," I'm sweating now. "Then what does she say."

"She says that she likes it when men touch her tits and she really likes it when they lick her nipples."

"Uh hum," this is my job. "Go on."

63

"She wants me to suck on them, she tells me that she would really like it if I ran my tongue around her nipples until they were hard."

"Yes." I work for the government.

"And then she tells me that when her nipples are hard, her pussy gets wet. She likes to touch herself when she's talking to me. She touches her vagina right when we're talking. She tells me that she wishes I could touch her. I tell her that I wish I could touch her too."

"Go on." Do you think the government knows what I do?

"Then she tells me that she wants me to get my cock out of my pants and play with it. She asks me to tell her when it's nice and hard. Then she says that she wants to ride on my cock. She says it would feel sooo good inside her."

"Um hum." I don't think they have any idea what I do.

"That's when it usually happens, the stuff comes out of my penis."

"And that feels good?" It takes years of training to learn to ask incredibly stupid questions.

"Yes it does."

"Then you hang up?"

"No."

"No?!" I'm surprised, I also decide never to use any of the phones in the office again.

"No, that's when the good stuff starts to happen."

"Good stuff! What good stuff?" This guy is an animal. I'm spent just hearing about it. What more could happen?

"That's when she stops talking dirty and starts talking nice to me. She tells me that she misses me when I don't call and that she

64

worries about me sometimes. She said that she looks forward to talking to me, that I am one of the favorite guys that call her. She told me once, I don't think that she was supposed to, that she had to make money because her husband left her. She asked me to tell her about my job, I kind of lied cause I didn't want her to know that I didn't make much money. I haven't talked to her for a few days and I really miss her."

Good stuff indeed. Part of the call was to meet sexual needs and part to meet emotional needs.

He had no friends. No one he could call when lonely. No one but a woman named Kristie with whom he could spend some time.

## PLAIN LANGUAGE

• People with disabilities often live lives of loneliness and quiet desperation.

• People who don't feel loved or loveable are ripe for exploitation.

• Creating a means for people with disabilities to learn how to meet affectional needs is the next great question.

## AFFECTIONAL NEEDS

A while back I did some work with male and female prostitutes who had a developmental disability. Working with the women was much harder than the men. The men liked the money, the perceived power, the camaraderie with the other hustlers and the autonomy. The women, however, liked those things but the major reason they sold themselves was to earn the affection of their boyfriends. It was much easier to get the men off the street because one can compete with the pragmatics of hustling. The women were impossible because they felt that they would never be loved by anyone else. One stated quite adamantly that no one ever loved her before so why should she think anyone would love her again. If she had to endure sex with men she didn't like to get affection from a man she loved, so be it.

## TAKING RESPONSIBILITY

All these people have been served by our system and we need to take responsibility for what we have done. People with disabilities have a history of having sexuality denied and their hearts disregarded. We have responded to loving with policy. We have responded to affection with punishment. We have responded to tenderness with restrictions. We have created a world wherein it is better to get beaten by a pimp that cares for you than live in a system that dehumanizes you. We have created a world wherein a man could live with other people with disabilities for his entire life and end up at forty-six, friendless and masturbating on a telephone with a complete stranger. These are ugly truths, but they are truths.

## *WHAT YOU CAN DO ABOUT IT*

• Challenge orthodoxy. If you work in an agency that has decided that disabled people should never be in social situations with one another, speak up. I was leading a workshop for an agency and I mentioned that people with disabilities need to have a wide range of friends including other people with disabilities. I stated that the idea that the public might be uncomfortable seeing a group of people with disabilities having dinner together is a reason to forbid a social outing for friends is archaic, racist and cruel. I went on to say that the issue was choice. For us to write a philosophy or policy that restricts the freedom of association is a violation of civil liberties. Afterwards, a young male staff brought his supervisor up to me and demanded that we all talk about it.

I was told that he worked in a group home wherein the clients, who used to go out to dinner on pay day, had been told that they could no longer go out together. Why? Their staff had been to training and learned that bigotry was acceptable and as such they restricted these men's access to a pleasant evening together once every two weeks. He protested, so did I, policy changed.

• It is pretty hard to develop a love for others if you are taught that you are worthless.

• Any policy that teaches a person with a disability to hate, despise or avoid others with disabilities is a form of emotional abuse.

- It is impossible to feel free when someone tells you where you can go, what you can do and with whom you can associate.

This is controversial because there is such a strong belief that people with disabilities should never be seen in groups, that any challenge is seen as a crime. I understand the genesis of the problem. For years people with disabilities were jailed for being who they were and were only allowed to be "With Their Own Kind." This was a travesty. True. But now to turn around and say that people with disabilities can never be with others with disabilities is doing the same thing. Both points of view focus on the disability as being the reason there is an issue at all. For me, personally, I can't understand why everyone can't see that the issue is that *we forced them into groups* and now *we are forcing them apart.* The issue is FORCE.

- It is none of y/our business who people with disabilities hang around with.

- Closing organizations and opportunities for people with disabilities to get together is inappropriate. Special Olympics should close when people with disabilities no longer want to attend. Our opinion is irrelevant.

- Develop a system that respects relationships. There is no point in doing sex education, or any of the suggestions that follow if people with disabilities are prohibited from engaging in appropriate sexual behaviour at home. Enough said.

- See prejudice and deal with it. Everyone in human services can tell stories of communities that did not welcome people with disabilities. There must be thousands of petitions out there which attest to the fact that people don't want people with disabilities in their neighbourhoods. We all have responded by trying to educate our communities, our families and our friends about people with disabilities in order to calm their fears. This is laudable.

However, when we hear someone we support say, "I don't like people with disabilities. I don't want to be around them. I would never ever want to be seen with someone like that." We often leap with joy and a sense of accomplishment. Why? When these sentiments are stated by a person with a disability we see that we have achieved the ultimate. We have "normalized" them to hate people with disabilities just like the regular community member!

I was at a conference here in Canada when someone approached me after a talk that I gave wherein I advocated for the right of people with disabilities to have friends with disabilities. This man was a reasonable man and he wanted to let me know that he understood why I said what I did. He cautioned me though that while he understood what I was saying, others wouldn't. Others would use my words as a means of continuing segregation. I asked him if I had made it clear that I was saying that people with disabilities should have a full range of choices. Yes, he understood that but he was afraid that others wouldn't have. Right, he was the only bright person in the audience. I have since discovered that anyone who holds a viewpoint believes that those that oppose them are simply stupid. They usually can't or won't understand that there are several sides to each question. Often all sides are equally right and equally wrong.

He then gave me an example of a woman with a disability who didn't like the company of others with disabilities. This woman apparently only liked the company of others without disabilities. He presented her to me as if she was an example of what could be done, she had, in his eyes anyway, transcended her disability. I responded by telling him that I knew a woman who didn't like the company of other women. She only liked to socialize with men and when having to get together with women she would become anxious and depressed. I asked him what I should do about it. He didn't get the point and said that she clearly had a problem. Right, she does. So does the woman with a disability. Hating others like yourself, is hating yourself.

We need to educate people with disabilities about people with disabilities. We need to encourage them to accept themselves and others like them. We need to put as much energy into teaching people with disabilities that they have value as we do any community member.

\*     \*     \*

68

## SEX EDUCATION

Main Message: SEX IS GOOD

This may be considered an odd sentiment in a book about the sexual victimization of people with developmental disabilities. Yet it may be one of the most important points. The message that "SEX IS GOOD" is a radical counterpoint to what people with disabilities have been told about sex. It also stands in stark contrast to what people with disabilities have experienced in their sexuality.

You will note that this book has not done a numerical presentation regarding the abuse of people with disabilities. It has not done so because others present those facts with much more clarity than I could ever do. Even so, I weighed out the merits of putting in the numbers. Then I read a quote that has stuck with me:

The death of one is a tragedy. The death of millions is a statistic.

I was afraid that reading the numbers would cause people to quote them rather than think of individual people. Even so, there is one statistic that I would like you to think about here in relation to sex education. If you add the number of people with disabilities who have been sexually victimized to the number of people with disabilities who have been punished for appropriate sexual behaviour you would have 100% of adults with disabilities alive today. Therefore, every person you work with has had their bodies assaulted or their hearts attacked. EVERY PERSON.

For these individuals, the message that sex is good is a radical one indeed. It can also be a healing one.

At home one night I received a call from one of the women who worked in our department. She was very distressed. I had never heard her in such turmoil. She was insistent that I pick up a case that had been referred to her as she felt the issue was not behaviour but was more in the area of sexuality. I asked her what the referral was for and she told me that it was for a woman of about fifty who engaged in "genital self-injury." I told her that she should talk to me in the morning and we could put her on the wait list for service. She was adamant that this woman not wait. She said that this woman has waited for years and it had to stop. She began to cry and told me that she had just witnessed something so disturbing that she was herself bruised by the experience.

Before I could protest that I already had a caseload that was full to overflowing she told me that the behaviour was low frequency and only happened at home. It would take many hours of observation to see the behaviour. She just wanted me to see it so that we could talk about it at least. I said that I could drop into the woman's group home a couple of evenings a week and hopefully then see the behaviour. By the way, what was the behaviour? She said that she didn't want to tell me, that I had to see it. All the staff in the home were instructed not to tell me about the behaviour.

I went to visit the home and met a very nice, quite, almost placid woman. She seemed, for the most part, to be at peace with herself. I couldn't imagine her engaging in "genital self-injury." It took a few weeks of observation for me to be there when it happened. After dinner a few of us were in watching television. She sat in her favourite chair which she sunk into letting the arms embrace her. Then there was an aura in the room. Something changed and then she did it. Her body changed, she arched her back, her facial features became distorted and her hand formed into a claw. She opened her legs as wide as they could go and she started screaming, "JESUS!!! JESUS!!! JESUS!!!" while ripping at her vulva through her clothing. The force was such that before she finished, blood seeped through her clothing and onto the chair. When done she fell back sobbing into the waiting arms of the chair. Then she curled herself into a ball and tried to sink into the warmth.

I was stunned. I have never seen anything quite so ugly. This was clearly more than a self injurious behaviour. This was punishment. An investigation into her past led to the discovery that she had reported being raped by a male staff who denied any charges. Years ago, she told someone of being hurt and was disbelieved. Years ago, she was counselled about the sin of lying. Years ago, her parents came in to talk to her about her sexual behaviour, it seems they were told that she had had sex with one of the men with disabilities in her

70

home. It seems that they were told their daughter was promiscuous and couldn't be trusted. It seems that they were told that their daughter was a liar. It seems that they were lied to. They then sat down with her and as gently as they could tried to explain sexuality to their daughter. They told her that the feelings that she had between her legs were messages from Satan. When she felt those feelings she was to call on Jesus for help and he would save her.

Years later a woman, a victim of an assault, is praying for God to take away any sexual feelings she has. For this woman to learn that "SEX IS GOOD" is more than education, it is therapy. She needs to understand that the same God to whom she cries to for help created us all to have feelings that are warm and pleasurable. She needs to understand that those feelings are a gift from that God. She needs to understand that she has been heard and believed. She needs to understand that it wasn't her vagina's fault that she was assaulted.

## LOOKING AT THE LIES

People with disabilities have learned lies about sexuality. These need to be addressed in any form of sex training. It has always been my belief that sex education is more sex therapy than it is education because it is a process that does more than teach facts. Done properly, it is a process that changes lives. Let's look at two of the most damaging lies that people have learned and alternate messages that must be given.

*Lie #1:* Sex is dirty and people who want to have sex are bad. The number of people with disabilities who have learned that all sex is bad is astronomical. Please don't think I am solely talking about history. Yesterday, I got a call from Debbie Richards to tell me about a boy that she was doing a sexuality assessment on and that he had already, just into puberty, learned that his body was bad and that sex was a horrible thing.

Healthy Message #1: SEX IS GOOD. Your body is a wonderful thing. It can give you pleasure. It can give pleasure to others. Your body is the same as everyone else's. All people feel sexual. All people have genitals that give them pleasure.

*Lie #2:* You shouldn't have sex because you will have a baby that's like you. This is the most horrible message of all. This harkens back to the eugenics movement when the world tried to eradicate itself of people with disabilities. Let me tell you that if you believe, down in your heart of hearts, that the world would be better off without people with disabilities in it, then get out of this field. I make no apologies for the strength of that statement. A belief that the only solution is the final solution makes you dangerous.

Healthy Message #2: SEX IS GOOD. You have the capacity to create life. This is a very big responsibility. It is, however, your choice. Your baby will probably be born without a disability but even if it has one, then it will grow up to be a loving person like you are. Parenting is one of the biggest choices that people make and you need to know all the facts before you make that decision.

## WHAT NEEDS TO BE TAUGHT
## TO INCREASE ABILITY TO PROTECT SELF
## FROM SEXUAL ASSAULT

1: Vocabulary. People need to know the names for all of their body parts and they need to know what function they serve. Please teach accurately. The name for female genitalia is most often taught incorrectly. Vulva, not vagina, is the name for female genitalia.

2: Pleasure. People need to know that they have parts of their body that give enormous amounts of pleasure. They need to know that this pleasure is a good thing and that their bodies were made to give pleasure. This is not an opinion, just note that the clitoris is the only organ of the body that exists for the sole purpose of giving pleasure. Our "Maker" is trying to communicate something and the clitoris is the clue.

3: Context. People need to know that the giving and receiving of sexual pleasure belongs in the context of a loving relationship. That both people need to agree. People need to know that when two people agree to have sex it is a very special relationship that means that they trust one another with their body and with their heart.

72

4: Responsibility. People need to know some basic facts about pregnancy. Women don't get pregnant from getting married. (Even if it often seems that way.) Pregnancy is a choice that both people make. If people are to learn about sex they also have to learn about responsible choices.

5: Facts. Disease has become an increasing concern. You will note that pregnancy and disease are presented separately. I have seen some classes wherein they have been taught together as if pregnancy is a sexually transmitted disease! Teaching about disease, particularly AIDS, has been difficult. The fact that risky sexual behaviour could lead to death has been a concept that many of our clients just didn't believe. When investigating why such an important message was not getting through, we discovered something awful. We have found that many people with disabilities have been lied to so much about their bodies that they just don't believe the facts about AIDS and other STD's. Telling someone that sex without a condom could lead to HIV and AIDS sounds a lot like, "If you masturbate it will fall off," or "If you have sex God will punish you." As a result we have had to change our teaching about disease. We now teach from the point of view of "LOVE" not death. If you love someone, you care for them and want to keep them healthy. This is a fact.

6: SEX IS GOOD AND IF IT ISN'T GOOD IT ISN'T SEX.

*     *     *

## PRIVACY AWARENESS

Main Message: PRIVACY IS GOOD

Privacy is a misunderstood concept. Not just by people with disabilities but by their care providers as well. How many meetings do you go to wherein people discuss a client's entire life, right in front of them? I have been in meetings and watched as a young man with a developmental disability has comfortably listened to a staff discuss the fact that she was aware that he masturbated to ejaculation because of the mess on the sheets. This same man has a problem with discriminating public and private places. SURPRISE!! SURPRISE!!!

Teaching privacy has been pulled out of the sex education curriculum and emphasized here because it is important to see that while sex education gives the vocabulary with which to report sexual abuse, privacy awareness teaches the concept that allows a person to understand violation. If you don't understand that your body is yours and no one can touch it without your permission, then you simply accept what happens to it as being part of what it is to be powerless. Once people understand that there is a rule that says our bodies are special and that we make the decision about who touches us, it is possible to conceptualize abuse.

Teaching about privacy is dangerous. This is the section of sex education that is taught most carefully. Sitting and explaining that all of our bodies are private but that there are some places on our bodies that are both special and private is one thing. But explaining that when someone touches our genitals they are touching a special place that is really private and that we have to agree to be touched there, is quite another. This is often the moment that the individual realizes that father \ aunt \ staff is an abuser. This can be incredibly emotional. As sex educators we are very careful in teaching this because this one concept can change a person's world forever. While this change, if it leads to increased safety, is good, it will be painful for a person to reconceptualize all that has happened to them. It should be noted that it has been our experience that the reporting of sexual abuse happens more during this section of teaching than any other.

The question that is probably popping into your mind right now is, "How could it be that people with disabilities can reach adulthood without understanding basic privacy?" That's an easy one and the answer is simple, "We didn't teach it." The more difficult question is "What do we do about this?" Well I didn't really have an answer either so, I went to experts.

## WHAT NEEDS TO BE TAUGHT
## TO INCREASE ABILITY TO PROTECT SELF
## FROM SEXUAL ASSAULT

1. Teach privacy by doing privacy. I held a meeting with a group of staff from an amazing group home. The staff were genuinely

committed to the people they serve and tried their level best to treat people with respect. What was amazing was that management was truly supportive of their front line staff and gave them the opportunity to provide excellent service. The first time I heard Jean Edwards speak, she talked about the routine violation of privacy that occurs in the provision of service. I was stunned and perplexed. She was right, in the provision of intimate care we can become desensitized to what we are doing and therefore destroy the concept of privacy for people with disabilities. I returned and when meeting with this group of staff I told them of Jean's presentation and they were as bewildered as myself as to how we could have all missed this as it seemed so obvious.

They took up the challenge. They were going to build privacy into their house. When I came back a week later, here is what they had done:

Get Permission: Before they provided any intimate care from helping with dressing, assisting with toileting, they asked. They felt that before they touched someone they should at least ask. For the one individual who was non-verbal they would ask for permission to help her on the toilet and wait until she turned to their voice and recognized them before helping. Their rule became, ask first, touch second.

Restructure where possible: One man that they had been supervising in the mornings when he showered had learned that it was acceptable to wander the house naked. They realized that he had grown used to being seen naked because staff would sit and watch him in the shower and give him instructions while watching him naked in front of them. If they couldn't supervise full time they would leave the door open to the bathroom and pop in to check on him. They felt that this was unacceptable and made a simple change. They lowered the shower curtain so that they could still see his face and give him instructions but there was now a visual barrier.

Adapt if necessary: Where it was deemed necessary to leave the bathroom door open for a young woman who took longer to do her business (so what's a little euphemism among friends) and there were safety concerns, they did two things. First, they made a gown that she could wear when toiletting. This was like a hospital gown that tied at the back of the neck and the back could flare open. She would never again sit naked with the door open. The next thing they did was to put in a dutch door that would allow them to close the bottom half of the door and thereby create a greater sense of privacy than leaving the whole door open.

Private subjects are private: In programming or planning meetings it was decided that the clients would never be subjected to hearing a discussion of their hygiene or sexuality in front of a group of people. More than that they were never to hear their genitals, the functioning of their genitals, menstruation or anything else openly talked about in a public forum.

See trust as a process: They had initially thought that since a new staff had passed the interview, they could just start off working with people in the most intimate of situations. They attempted (as much as possible) to bring in a new staff differently. Staff who were long-standing would take over all intimate care until the new staff became known and trusted by the clients. The new staff would do things like assist with cooking or teach more public skills like vacuuming. Even so, the first time that the new staff was to provide any intimate care they would ask first.

Touch differently: Many of the staff had allowed their clients to give them bear hugs. This was slowly withdrawn because of a situation that happened which taught them why their method of touch was not only inappropriate but was teaching different things.

One of the women in their home had recently learned to travel on the transit system to and from work. This was a major accomplishment and was celebrated as such. When she started travelling on her own she developed a friendly relationship with the male bus driver on her route. We learned that she was totally appropriate in the development of her friendship with him. It began innocently enough with her getting on the bus and saying "Good Morning" and going to the back of the bus by the rear door as she had learned in her program. Over the course of several months the relationship between her and the bus driver developed to a warm albeit casual relationship.

She would sit at the front of the bus and talk with him. He told her that he always liked it when she got on because she always was smiling.

Then he told her he was going on vacation for two weeks and that he would bring her a post card of his holiday. She said she would miss him. This is all totally appropriate. It's what we want to happen out there. It is the point of integration. People meeting people and learning to like each other without need for interference from the social service system.

Then tragedy struck.

The Monday he returned from vacation she was so excited about him coming back and was thrilled about the post card she was going to get from him. She waited for the bus with great anticipation and when it came she was thrilled to see him driving. He waved to her as he pulled up. She had been recognized. When she got on the bus she saw the post card poking out through his uniform and was flooded with affection for him. What do you think she did? If you said that she hugged him, you would be wrong. A hug is a form of touch that both people have to agree to, if it isn't mutual it isn't a hug, it is an assault. She assaulted him with her affection. As she tried to grab him, he pushed her away and was quite angry with her.

He didn't give her the post card. He didn't speak much to her on the bus ride. He wasn't there the next day. She was devastated. When the transit system was called, the group home staff was informed that the driver was terrified that someone might witness her grab him and instead of seeing him as being attacked they may assume that he is the attacker. He is worried that accusations are going to be made about him because he was friendly to her. He has requested to drive a different route. The request was immediately granted.

Hold it! Just hold it! I know some of you are thinking that he over-reacted and was being unreasonable. I know some of you are thinking that what happened wasn't that serious. Well, it was. To think any less is to deny his victimization and her power to intrude. Just imagine if it was the other way around, that the driver had been a woman and the "hugger" had been a man with a developmental disability. Would you see the woman's fear as being extreme? Would you see the man's behaviour as being less than serious. Be careful about sexism.

This woman had few affectional skills. In fact, she had learned that one shows affection through touch and touch alone. She needs to learn that there are many ways to show affection and touch is just one of them. In fact, she had to learn that bear hugs are scary to people you don't know well and even many of those you do, don't like that kind of touch. The group home set about teaching staff how to show affection to their clients. Sometimes using an appropriate touch, but never a bear hug, sometimes by a word, sometimes a look, sometimes a smile, sometimes using proximity and tone of voice.

2. Teach accurately about the body. You will have figured out already that I am not a fan of teaching that there are only a few private parts of the body. I prefer to teach that all the body is private but that some parts of the body are special. The reason for this is that I have seen in my practice, people misbehaving more after sex education than before. One man, having learned that the private parts of a woman's body were her vagina (Vulva, the Word is Vulva, can we all say Vulva), her breasts and her bum. This man logically thought that all the rest of the body was then public. His victim didn't agree when he stroked her thigh on the bus!

More than creating the misconception in the mind of a person with a disability regarding the body as being basically public and having the person then act on that belief, this type of teaching gives a victimizer great access to the body of a person with a disability. If you think that your body is completely touchable with the exception of a few "hot spots" then you don't mind if a staff massages your back and sides. A rub on the leg, that's OK because it's public. Inner thigh, no concern here. Stomach, go ahead. You see the problem. Be careful, and if you insist on using the words, "private parts" then make sure they understand that the rest of the body is special too! Also be cautious of the term "pubic hair" more than one of the people I have taught couldn't say those words and instead used the words "public hair". This worried me enough to change and teach the words "adult hair".

*    *    *

## ABILITY TO NON COMPLY

Main Message: *NO!!* IS GOOD

This is a tough sell. Most people with disabilities who are adults have been taught that it is their job simply to do what they are told. As a result we have people with disabilities who believe that they never have any choice about what happens to them. We also then have staff who believe that a client who doesn't immediately follow through on a demand is a problem. Let me tell you a story from my days as a behavioural consultant. I like to tell people that I have worked with a cereal killer. This is his story.

Once upon a time there was a man with a developmental disability who was "known to dislike cold cereal". After fighting with him to try to get him to eat cold cereal they eventually gave up and would allow him to just eat toast in the morning. A small victory but a victory nonetheless. One morning a new staff started who did not know that this particular client didn't like cold cereal. He checked the menu and discovered that on Wednesday's it was, you got it, cold cereal. He poured the cereal and began making the toast as the residents got themselves up. This group home was pretty good about residents being involved in all aspects of their own care, but breakfast had traditionally been handled by staff. There was only one morning staff on, and in order to get everyone up and out on time, it was seen as more efficient to give the residents the job of getting ready and the staff the job of making breakfast.

When the cereal bigot arrived for breakfast and saw cold cereal at his place he told the staff that he didn't like cold cereal. The staff told him that cold cereal was on the menu and cold cereal would be eaten. The client thought maybe that the staff didn't hear. He stated again that he didn't like cold cereal. As he did so he sat down at his place and pushed the cereal away and pulled in the toast. The staff approached this non-compliant problem client and pushed the cereal in towards him and pulled the toast back. The difficult client was told that he could not eat the toast until he ate his cereal. At this point the client engaged in a "psychotic outburst of rage" and threw the cereal against the wall smashing the bowl into little pieces.

Hearing this story there are a number of things that are immediately evident. First, I would have thrown the cereal after the first order. Second, I would have thrown the cereal at the staff. Third, I would have demanded an apology for being treated so disrespectfully. Fourth, the problem person in the story is the staff. Even if the staff didn't know that the client didn't like cold cereal, he had been politely informed. This shouldn't have been an issue.

It was because we see almost every action of a client as a thing to be controlled. This is hugely problematic.

## PLAIN LANGUAGE

People who don't learn how to say no to small things can't say it to big things.

## PLAINER LANGUAGE

- People who can't say no to peas will never understand their right to say no to a penis.

## WHAT NEEDS TO BE TAUGHT TO INCREASE ABILITY TO PROTECT SELF FROM SEXUAL ASSAULT

1. Appropriate non-compliance skills. Non-compliance a skill? Absolutely it is. Teaching clients how to stick up for themselves is mandatory if they are ever going to be able to clearly say "No" when "No" is imperative. Every staff who is in contact with people with disabilities needs to gently determine if their clients either know how to refuse and if they will when necessary. Try this little exercise. Think of someone you support. Now imagine yourself standing next to them at a stove with a hot burner. Imagine telling them to touch it. Would they? Imagine raising your voice and demanding that they touch it. Would they? Tell them that if they don't touch it they are going to be in big, big trouble. Would they?

80

If you believe that your client would touch it, you have a problem. If you believe that your client wouldn't touch it but that it would be a difficult decision for them to defy you, you have a problem. If you believe that your client wouldn't touch it, but that they wouldn't tell another staff what you had tried to do, you have a problem.

Purposefully set up situations where a person with a disability has the opportunity to say "no". This is the only way to learn. Be very careful that you do not try this out by giving dangerous instructions. Pick things that are safe so that the individual is not confused about safety rules. Telling a person to run into traffic as a means of testing their non-compliance skills is very unwise.

2. To differentiate demands from choices. Too often people with disabilities are offered false choices. And when they choose wrongly they are made to change their mind. Look at this scene which happens so commonly as to be epidemic in human services.

It's outing night. The van is warming in the driveway. Everyone is ready to go but Yves. Yves, being Yves, is lounging on one of the chairs in front of the television. One of the staff approaches him and says, "Yves, do you want to go on the outing?" Note the staff asked a question. The staff implied that there was a choice here. Yves says, "No, thanks. I want to watch television." Note that Yves made a choice. Note that Yves understood that a choice had been offered. What is going to happen? Do you think Yves is going to go on that outing? You bet your booties he's going to go. More than that the staff is probably going to raise her voice and insist that he get going right now.

What is Yves learning?

"No," does not mean, "no". It's that simple. This happens probably hundreds of times a week to a person with a disability. I stress in my workshops for staff that they need to be very careful about offering a choice. Offer choices only where there is a choice. If it is a demand then make sure that it is seen as an issue with no choice. If it is a choice then make it a choice. More than that, if you mistakenly say, "Don't you want to do your dishes tonight?" and the client responds, "No" then you do them. Never cross a person's "no" when you have offered choice.

*　　*　　*

## SOMEONE WHO LISTENS

Main Message: SPEAKING IS GOOD

A while back I got a call from Linda Perry to talk to me about doing a workshop together. She had an idea. She wanted to hold a conference for people with disabilities and their care providers. The subject was to be the word "no" and its importance. It was to be structured such that the first morning session would be a joint session, then people with disabilities and their care providers would go to separate rooms. I would teach people with disabilities how, when and under what circumstances they could say "NO!" Linda would teach the care providers how to hear the word "NO!" Then we would get back together and the two groups would role play some of the skills they had learned.

We didn't expect the conferences to be such a hit. But we got huge numbers all over the province. Linda and I were stunned at the numbers and at the realization that care providers saw this as a need. We had joked that she and I would be alone in big halls because who would send a person with a disability to a conference to learn how to defy their care providers. We were delightfully wrong.

On one of the stops, a young woman with Down's Syndrome approached me just before lunch. She said that she wanted to say something to the group. I said that when we got back from lunch she could talk first thing. She said that she wanted to talk to everybody, the whole group. I asked her what she wanted to talk about. She said that she wanted to say it later. Well, I had spent the morning teaching people to speak up when they wanted something and here she was doing it. Sure, I said. I rushed to Linda. Did she know this young woman? No she did not. I told her that she had requested to speak in front of the entire audience. We agreed that it was her choice. This is a nation founded on the principle of free speech after all.

At second break, just before she was to speak, her mother and staff approached and thanked me for giving her the opportunity to speak. Anne's mother told me that this would be healing for her. HEALING??? I'm not sure I wanted healing to happen in front of 175 people. But the die was cast. I set up the microphone to be about Anne's height. She didn't want the microphone where it was. She wanted it placed on the large stage behind where Linda and I spoke. We moved the microphone.

Anne approached the microphone and spoke hesitantly because of a speech problem. She augmented her speech with sign when she got stuck. There in front of an audience of 175, a sixteen year old girl, with a developmental disability and a speech impediment, spoke. Her tone was hushed and the microphone broadcast the intimacy of her voice. She told the audience of being hurt by a man. She named her abuser. She told of going to the police. She told of going to court. She told of the imprisoning of the man who had hurt her. She told every person in the audience that they didn't have to take it. She told them that if someone was hurting them now that they could make it stop. She told them that they just had to tell. She spoke quietly but with conviction. And then she stopped.

She stood silently. As if observing a minute of silence for the death of her innocence. She did not leave. She began to cry. I wanted to help her, but she was alone at the microphone. I looked at her mother and wondered how proud she must feel of her daughter and how painful the experience must have been for her. As Anne stood and cried, I still thought that she had finished. But she had not. She then said, "But that's not what I wanted to say."

She then said that she got up in front of everyone because she wanted to thank her mother who believed her when she told. She wanted to thank her staff who took her to the police station. She wanted to thank her friends who were there for her all the way. She wanted to thank everyone who had listened to her. She cried. They cried. We cried. I cried. When she stepped back from the microphone 175 people stood and applauded her courage. A standing ovation for a hero.

A sixteen year old girl with a developmental disability understood. She understood the facts. The facts are simple. Given that she was a child. Given the fact that she had a disability. It's amazing anyone listened at all. Anne taught me that it didn't matter if people had sex education and all the vocabulary to report abuse. It doesn't matter if someone understands the concept of privacy and privacy violations. If there isn't someone there to listen and believe, it's all for nothing.

## WHAT NEEDS TO BE TAUGHT
## TO INCREASE ABILITY TO PROTECT SELF
## FROM SEXUAL ASSAULT

• Speak up.

### *WHAT YOU CAN DO*

• Listen up.

## WHAT ABOUT THOSE WHO DO NOT SPEAK?

We are linguistically arrogant. We have actually come to believe that if a person doesn't speak in words they don't speak at all. When I moved to Quebec a few years ago, I was aware that I was moving into a Francophone province and that since I didn't speak French I was not going to be allowed to work with people with disabilities in that province. I understood and applauded this as it makes sense to me that if you can't serve a person in their language then you shouldn't serve them.

Yet when I thought about it I realized that for many people who are non-verbal we make the assumption that this means that they are non-communicative. Nothing could be further from the truth. They speak the language of the body, of behaviours, of facial expressions and of physical gestures and movements. Everyone who works with a person that cannot speak knows that they still can communicate. The trouble is we respect our language and not theirs and as such we spend a lot of time trying to teach a person to communicate through standard patterns, speech, sign, or symbol and grade their ability to communicate by how they learn these standard patterns. While it is important that people with disabilities learn how to communicate, isn't it also important that the staff who support them be required to learn their language?

I refuse to work with anyone until a language dictionary is compiled that tells me how a person communicates emotions, desires, humour and other messages. I learned this the hard way. I was asked to do some counselling with a woman who was quite aggressive. They had tried programming and thought that maybe talking to her might help. Well, I was up to it so I went into a little office with her and began to chat. It was an initial meeting so nothing stressful was said. Out of the blue she kicked me hard. I got up feeling the bruise forming on my leg and left the room. When I told the staff what she had done, he said to me, "I'll bet just before she kicked you her lip trembled a bit." I acknowledged that it did. "Yeah," he said pleased with himself, "She always does that before she strikes out."

ALWAYS DOES THAT!

I want this information before I meet with someone.

Look at what happened from her perspective. She was upset, probably feeling caged in with this stranger, she warned me -USING HER LANGUAGE- that I was going to get hurt. She respected me enough to warn me. But I didn't know her language and I got what I deserved. I don't make this mistake any more. I don't look good in black and blue.

It is interesting to meet with staff and tell them that I want them to come up with a dictionary of a person's language. They usually approach the task as if it will take a couple of minutes and be only a paragraph long. What I find however is that usually hours later they have compiled a several page document that describes any number of concepts and messages that the person is quite capable of sending. A single exercise changes their view of a person forever. Instead of being seen as linguistically incompetent, the person is seen as a "LINGUISTIC MINORITY OF ONE." What a difference an attitude change makes.

This exercise has three benefits. First, it makes life a lot easier for the person with a disability. Before this is done they have to spend several months of training with new staff to teach them their language. Having it written down makes transition to new staff much easier. Second, it gives all staff access to information about a person's language. This makes it less likely that one staff will horde all the information and therefore have maximum power over the individual. Third, it creates a hostile environment for abusers. An abuser that comes to work in a place where staff are trained in the language of their clients had better be careful because staff have the capacity to read and understand slight changes in a person's demeanour or temperament.

*   *   *

## UNDERSTANDING OF PERSONAL RIGHTS

Main Message: RIGHTS ARE GOOD

It is important to recognize that all citizens have rights and that just because one is a resident of an agency, those rights have not been waived. People with disabilities need to be informed of what their rights are. I am dispensing with a long introduction here because I assume that if you live in a free society you understand the value of rights. If you have trouble understanding the importance of your rights because you are so used to having them, simply ask yourself, "Which of my rights would I willingly give up?" The right to vote? The right to free assembly? The right to freely express your religion? The right to freedom of speech? The right to a free press? The right to arm bears? Which of these would you willingly give up? If you are having difficulty deciding, then you are re-acquainted with the importance of civil liberties.

### WHAT NEEDS TO BE TAUGHT
### TO INCREASE ABILITY TO PROTECT SELF
### FROM SEXUAL ASSAULT

• The basic rights the individual has in the system. If the person is to be able to exercise their rights then they need to know what they are. If they are going to learn them then staff need to know what they are. An agency I worked with a few years ago had come up with a wonderful idea. They pulled front line staff together and asked them to develop a list of rights that all people with disabilities have within the agency. Then they asked them to come up with a list of restrictions on staff that clients needed to know about. Once this was done, one of the front line staff worked at illustrating with a simple picture each one of the rights and restrictions. Now in that agency every person with a disability has a booklet that describes their rights. They also invite in an external advocate to regularly review the booklet with their clients to ensure that they are doing what they set out to do, respect their rights.

• There is a movement of self-advocates aimed at lobbying for and protecting civil rights. The People First movement is aimed at giving people with disabilities a forum for meeting and discussing political and systemic issues. This movement is creating leaders. Every person with a disability needs to be aware of its existence and if there isn't a local group, they need to be able to contact them to set one up.

• The Creative Center in Visalia, California, has created a video called, "David's Discovery: A Story of Human Rights." It is not expensive and is a wonderful tool for teaching people about both their rights and the People First movement. I wrote about this video in my book "*i to I: Self Concept and People with Developmental Disabilities*", in 1990. Four years later, I still recommend it. The concept of rights is somehow timeless.

*    *    *

## HEALTHY SELF CONCEPT AND SELF CONFIDENCE

Main Message: I AM GOOD

If you are different, in any way, the world and the people in it seem to want to tell you that you have no value. One day, in Vancouver, I was walking down Davie Street. It was the first day of my weekend off and the sun broke through clouds that had spent the week with me. It had been a good week. Linda and I had done training of several hundred people with disabilities in their rights. We had seen healing. We watched people's spines stiffen. We watched caregivers begin the trek from domination to guidance and it felt

87

good.  Really, really good.  A new vegetarian, I had lunched at Doll and Penny's restaurant where they served a mean veggie burger.  I was going back to the hotel before heading out on my usual "Saturday in Vancouver" walk.

For a second my defenses were down.  Momentarily, I thought the world was changing.  In the briefest of seconds I forgot who I was and just felt good about what I was doing.

It is dangerous for fat people to ever forget that we are an abomination in the eyes of the thin.  The word "Fatso!" was flung at me.  Even though it has long since lost it's power to shame me, the hate that it comes wadded in still impacts.  Here I was, feeling like I had accomplished something, and someone could still push all the way through my defenses and denigrate me.  I kept on walking.  I am well trained in the art of ignoring the hateful.  Sitting down in my hotel room, I was angry with myself.  How could I have let that happen?  What a fool.

What is the difference between the words, Fatso, Faggot, Nigger, Kike, Retard, Spic, Bitch?  There is none.  Those who live with the words know the importance of developing a firm sense of self in order to survive.  This is no less true for people with disabilities.  They, like others who have been despised in our society have been denied access, denied service, denied jobs, they have even been denied their liberty.  Yet they are luckier than most, they have you.  You have bothered to read this book.  You clearly care.  Make a pledge that you will work to make your clients stronger in self and firmer in pride, every single day you work with them.  You have the power to teach skills.  Teach the ability to self heal.  Teach the capability of self evaluation. Teach the skill of self love.

## WHAT NEEDS TO BE TAUGHT
## TO INCREASE ABILITY TO PROTECT SELF
## FROM SEXUAL ASSAULT

The sense that, "I matter."

Make that true by word, by action and by attitude.

## SUMMARY

You will note that the ring of safety is designed to be a permeable set of skills and defenses. It neither teaches that everyone is dangerous nor does it teach that all sexual feelings are bad. Instead, it teaches the difference between love and hate, abuse and consent, fists and palms. The goal of the ring of safety is to give the person with a disability a means of allowing love, in all it's glory, entry while keeping potential abusers at bay.

# EPILOGUE

## AN EXALTATION OF LARKS

During the training he hid. At least he tried to. He sat holding on to his girlfriend's hand and leaning slightly behind her. He watched us warily, not quite believing what was being said. He was hearing, maybe for the first time, that he had rights, that he was a person worthy of respect and that he had the right to say "No". It was interesting to watch how he scrutinized the face of the trainer looking for duplicity. He found none.

He said nothing to any of us for the first four hours of training. He never participated in any way but to watch the trainers and the others. When the subject was feelings, he made his move. His hand rose slightly. This was significant. All participants were told that we would not call on them unless they indicated that they wanted to participate. Now when people were discussing what scared them, his hand rose almost imperceptibly. The trainer, bright and fast, saw him. She asked, "Yes Bob, What scares you?"

"My mother." It was a statement. She followed without probing saying that many times family members could scare us.

"She swears at me. She says she is going to hit me. I don't like that, it makes me scared." His feeling was acknowledged and some of the other people with disabilities listened to him and told him that it was wrong for people to swear.

The training went on, but Bob, having spoken and aired a concern had been validated. The next few hours was like watching a flower grow on time lapse photography. A man who hid at the beginning was now up doing role plays. It was gratifying to see what could happen when people are informed of their rights, have their feelings validated and to do so in a safe place full of people who understand what it is to be disabled. The training ended.

A success.

As we were winding up, one of the trainers approached me and told me that Bob's mother had just showed up. She decided to come and see him and wanted him to go with her. She was waiting in the front hall. Bob was terrified. It must have seemed to him like she had some extra sense and had shown up just after he had spoken unkindly of her. His fear grew and he ran and hid behind his girl-friend. She was not afraid and stated quite plainly that she and he had made plans for dinner and his mother showing up was quite inconvenient.

Bob would not go out to the front hall. He refused to move. He didn't say a word he just hid. Clearly Bob was uncomfortable with all of us around and I suggested that he stay where he is and his mother could come in and talk with him. We would go to the far end of the room so that they would have privacy. When his mother came in she was walking on air she was so mad. Her approach to him was anything but loving and the tone of her voice left little to interpret, he was to go with her and go right now.

Then it happened. He took a breath, filled his lungs, opened his mouth and said, "No." The shock on his mother's face mirrored his own. Truth were known, I'd guess that Bob surprised himself more than he surprised his mother. Her anger escalated and she swore at him telling him that he had better move right now. There were 120 eyes in that room watching the scene. Sixty people with disabilities that had spent a day together learning how to say "No." They had heard Bob speak of his fear. They had heard us acknowledge his fear. They turned to us and gave us a look that said, "Do something staff-like."

We didn't. It was hard but we didn't.

When they realized that we would not save him, that he was on his own with his mother, something happened. They saw the unfair-ness of the situation. They saw her treat him disrespectfully and in a twinkling of an eye they were not sixty separate people with indi-vidual views of the world. They, like all living beings when one of their own is attacked, banded together against the danger. They were a Parliament of Owls, a Murmuring of Starlings, a Pride of Lions. They were more than a Community of People, they were a Family of

Friends. They breathed their disapproval at first. Then they spoke, one at a time but as one, "You can't talk to him like that. It's not nice. It's not fair."

Bob's mom was losing. He was not budging. And everyone who saw, knew that she was in the wrong. She left the room and paced outside. Just then a staff from his group home showed up, spoke briefly with Bob's mother and then and came and found him. Bob was told that his mother was tired of waiting and he was to go with her, RIGHT NOW. Bob's eyes filled with tears and he said almost inaudibly, "But I want to go for dinner with my girlfriend. We had plans." The group home staff leaned over him and told him that he had to do what he was told and he was being told to go with his mother.

Bob's eyes hardened. He had said it once and since once wasn't enough he said it again.

"No."

In the face of someone who openly and defiantly says that they were not going to do what they didn't want to do everyone else became impotent. What were they going to do? Before there was time for making a decision Bob went out and told his mother that he had made plans. If she wanted to see him that would be fine but she had to call first. She was lost. The power shift had been too swift and too complete. She quietly got in that car and drove away. The staff, also with no options got in the van and drove away.

Bob went out with his girlfriend for dinner.

Oh, I am not naive. Bob has a long walk ahead of him. He has many battles to fight to be considered a man capable of making decisions. He will lose some, he will win some. Life is messy. There are no tidy endings to any story. But Bob signified something important.

The battle has begun.

# FURTHER READING

*Baladerian, N.J. (1991)* The Sexual Assault Survivor's Handbook: For People with Developmental Disabilities and Their Advocates, Saratoga: R & E Publishers


*Brown, G.T., Carney, P., Cortis, J.M., Metz, L.L., Petrie, A.M. (1994)* Human Sexuality Handbook: Guiding People Toward Positive Expressions of Sexuality, Springfield: The Association for Community Living


*Caprio-Orsini, C. (in press)* Visual Reality: People with Developmental Disabilities Healing from Trauma through Art, Eastman: Diverse City Press


*Hingsburger, D. (1990)* I Contact: Sexuality and People with Developmental Disabilities, Mountville: Vida Publishing


*Hingsburger, D. (1990)* i to I: Self Concept and People with Developmental Disabilities, Mountville: Vida Publishing


*Hingsburger, D. (1993)* I Openers: Parents Ask Questions about Sexuality and their Children with Developmental Disabilities, Vancouver, Family Support Insititute Press


*Sobsey, D. (1994)* Violence and Abuse in the Lives of People with Disabilities: The End of Silent Acceptance?, Baltimore: Paul H. Brookes

*Sobsey, D., Gray, S., Wells, D., Pyper, D. and Reimer-Heck, B. (1991)* Disability, Sexuality, and Abuse: An Annotated Bibliography, Baltimore: Paul H. Brookes


*Ticoll, M. (1992)* No More Victims: A manual to Guide Families and Frineds in Preventing the Sexual Abuse of People with a Mental Handicap, North York: The Roeher Institute


*Ticoll, M. (1992)* No More Victims: A manual to Guide Counsellors and Social Workedrs in Addressing the Sexual Abuse of People with a Mental Handicap, North York: The Roeher Institute


*Ticoll, M. (1992)* No More Victims: A Manual to Guide Police in addressing the Sexual Abuse of People with a Mental Handicap, North York: The Roeher Institute


*Valenti-Hein, D. (1993)* The Sexual Abuse Interview for the Developmentally Disabled, Sacamento: James Stanfield Publications

# ABOUT THE AUTHOR

• Dave Hingsburger is an internationally known author and lecturer. He has published numerous articles and books on issues related to sexuality and people with developmental disabilities. He is a contributing editor of the Habilitative Mental Healthcare Newsletter and sits on the national advisory board of the Sexual Information and Education Council of Canada. Most importantly, however, Dave continues as a therapist and consultant to people with disabilities at York Central Hospital Sexuality Clinic.

# ABOUT DIVERSE CITY PRESS

Diverse City Press has set itself the goal of publishing clearly written and affordable material in the field of developmental disability. Just Say Know! is Diverse City's first book to be followed by an exciting new book by Cynthia Caprio-Orsini and Dave has promised a new book by the end of the year. We, at Diverse City, are open to hearing comments regarding any of our books. Too, we are open to receiving manuscripts from people who work directly with people with disabilities.

Transcontinental
PRINTING
MÉTROLITHO

Printed in Canada